Contents

Acknowledgments

For all those in the kitchens of Camp Denali and North Face Lodge. You make them warm, creative places to work. Because of you, the recipe cache continues to grow.

For Wally and Jerri, whose vision and commitment to excellence continue to inspire us all.

— L. C.

Preface

For centuries, elevated wooden platforms similar to the one on the cover were used to protect dried fish and game meat from bears, wolverines, and other animals. Borrowing this Native tradition, many an Alaska pioneer constructed a storage cabin on stilts, or "cache," even before building a place to live.

More than fifty years ago, Camp Denali pioneered its in-depth active learning adventures in Denali National Park. Gone are the days when its cache stored the canned corned beef that formed the base for an evening's creative dinner entrée. Even since 1979, when the first edition of *A Cache of Recipes* was published, changing palates and gradually increasing availability of fresh ingredients have influenced our cuisine.

Important traditions have endured. Uniquely situated with unparalleled views of Mount McKinley, Camp Denali and North Face Lodge are still committed to excellence and to creating a sense of community and place for visitors to Denali National Park. For more than half a century, the camaraderie built among guests and staff continues to be enhanced by food that nourishes, delights the eye, and pleases the palate.

Welcome to this new storehouse of recipes by my daughter-in-law, Laura, and illustrated by another staff associate and artist, Sara Tabbert. It's a cache of new creations prepared with today's flair. Preserved in the back are a few of our timeless classics.

— Jerryne Cole

Introduction

More than fifty years ago, the awe-inspiring panorama of Mount McKinley and the Alaska Range beckoned Morton and Virginia Wood and Celia Hunter to homestead land and establish a wilderness retreat in what is now the wilderness heart of Denali National Park. Their early promotional literature best described their vision for Camp Denali:

With wilderness fast disappearing in the first 48 states, Alaska offers the last large, unspoiled outdoor laboratory for the study and appreciation of undisturbed nature. Here you may still have the experience of the frontiersmen and explorers who first gazed on unbroken prairies, unharnessed rivers and undiminished wildlife.

Camp Denali's founders started with a few tent-frame cabins equipped with bunk beds, sleeping bags, and Yukon stoves. Today, after almost three decades of ownership by the Cole family, log and frame cabins dot Camp Denali's hillside and nearby North Face Lodge provides the ambience of a North Country inn. We continue to generate our own electricity, maintain our own access roads and trails, and do our own building design, construction, and interior decorating, including quilts handcrafted by staff. We also operate two well-equipped kitchens, a bakery, a large greenhouse, and a natural underground refrigeration system.

To this day, stewardship of the natural world and commitment to quality define Camp Denali and North Face Lodge. The personalized experiences of these two destinations blend serious appreciation of nature with camaraderie and a sense of community. Their extraordinary locations, small sizes, and family ownership command a strong sense of place.

I first started washing dishes and assisting the cooks in the kitchens of Camp Denali and North Face Lodge in 1994. It was my first experience in professional food service settings. I was enthralled with these warm, welcoming places of creative energy, humor, and satisfying hard work. Staff and guests continually passed through, sharing stories of their days as they munched on warm, fresh-baked cookies. With extraordinary effort these places produced amazing cuisine in an exceedingly remote location. Staples were laid in at the beginning of the season. Menus were carefully crafted to coincide with the weekly delivery of perishables transported from the park entrance. That summer I was introduced to the importance of food utilization, recipe adjustments, nutrition, organic ingredients, and seasonal and regional cooking. My world was in perfect harmony when I trod the path to my little log cabin as the setting sun cast its pink glow on the snow-clad peaks of the Alaska Range.

Years have passed. I have since earned a degree from the New England Culinary Institute and a master certificate for confections from the Ritz Escoffier L'École de Gastronome in Paris. I was lucky enough to fall in love with an exceptional man who has helped foster the vision of Camp Denali and North Face Lodge. I continue to cook, and my role as food service coordinator also enables me to cultivate the appreciation of culinary arts in others. It is my hope that the kitchens of Camp Denali and North Face Lodge continue to provide such inspiration in the shadow of Denali. This book is a collection of some of our favorite recipes. We hope you enjoy them.

Breakfast

Day breaks. As the sun pushes higher in the sky, the Alaska Range blushes with alpenglow. The kitchen crew has been busy. When the coffee is hot and the final preparations for the meal are underway, the breakfast cook steps out on the porch and rings the bell, welcoming guests to a hot cup of coffee and the start of a new day in Denali.

Cereals

In the shadow of the "Great One," we awaken most mornings to a chill in the air, so we always start our day with hot, cooked cereal complemented by homemade yogurt and fresh fruit.

Sandra & Hap loved this.

Peppy Kernels

Our own blend of organic grains and seeds makes a nutritious, filling hot cereal. Any leftover cooked cereal tastes great in bread. Just mix in up to 1 cup of cereal when you start adding the flour.

Yield: 13 cups uncooked cereal

4 cups rolled oats
2 cups wheat flakes
2 cups bulgur wheat
1 cup sesame seeds
1 cup flax seeds
1 cup millet seeds
1 cup bran
1 cup wheat germ

Combine all ingredients, mix well, and store in a tightly covered container. Use 2 parts liquid (such as water or apple juice) to 1 part uncooked cereal.

Yield: 1 serving

½ cup uncooked cereal
1 cup liquid (such as water or apple juice)

Place the liquid into a heavy-bottomed saucepan. Add a bit of butter and a dash of salt. Add the grains and reduce the heat to a simmer. Cover and cook for 30 minutes. Serve with your favorite toppings.

Maple-Pecan Wheat Barley Flakes

Create a new flavor by using any type of nuts you prefer in this warming cereal. For the ultimate in decadence, top this cereal with freshly whipped cream.

Yield: 6 cups cooked cereal

3½ cups apple cider
1 tablespoon butter
⅛ teaspoon salt
¼ cup maple syrup
1 tablespoon vanilla extract
1 cup wheat flakes
1 cup barley flakes
1 cup pecans, toasted and chopped

In a large, heavy-bottomed saucepan, combine the cider, butter, and salt. Bring to a boil, reduce the heat, and add the maple syrup, vanilla, and wheat and barley flakes. Cover and cook over low heat for 30 minutes. Stir in chopped pecans and serve with your favorite toppings.

Apple-and-Tart-Cherry Scotch Oats

Also known as Irish oatmeal, this hot cereal has a particularly creamy texture due to milling.

Yield: 6 cups cooked cereal

2 cups apple cider
2 cups whole milk
⅓ cup honey
⅛ teaspoon salt
1 tablespoon butter
1 teaspoon vanilla extract
1 Granny Smith apple
2 cups steel-cut Scotch oats
½ cup dried tart or sour cherries
1 teaspoon ground cinnamon
1 teaspoon ground ginger
⅛ teaspoon ground nutmeg

In a large, heavy-bottomed saucepan, combine the cider, milk, honey, salt, butter, and vanilla. Bring to a boil over medium-high heat. Core, peel, and dice the apple. Reduce the heat and add the oats, cherries, cinnamon, ginger, and nutmeg. Cover and cook over low heat for 30 minutes. Apple should be added for the last 15 minutes of cooking time. Serve with your favorite toppings.

Yogurt

At Camp Denali we are never without a store of yogurt in the larder. We use it in everything from salad dressings to fresh herb cheese to baked goods. It is also our favorite accompaniment for hot cereal. We had this with out hot cereal

If you don't have an incubator, transfer the warm milk/starter mixture to a clean container with a tight-fitting lid. Place the container in a warm water bath (between 110°F and 120°F). Let it sit, maintaining the water temperature, for 5 hours, or until it reaches the desired consistency.

Yield: 4 cups

4 cups milk (any kind)
⅓ cup starter (some purchased plain yogurt or some of your last batch)

In a heavy-bottomed saucepan over medium heat, bring the milk to 180°F. Take care not to burn it or to let it boil over. Remove from the heat and allow the milk to cool to 110°F. When cool, mix in the starter. Transfer to a yogurt incubator and incubate for 5 hours or until firm. Refrigerate.

Granola

Homemade granola is such a satisfying treat. A mouthwatering aroma fills the kitchen as it bakes. This always makes a great gift, and you can customize it by adding dried fruits of your choice.

Yield: 14 cups

½ cup vegetable oil
1 cup honey
1 tablespoon vanilla extract
2 teaspoons almond extract
2 tablespoons water
7 cups rolled oats
2 cups wheat germ
2 cups flaked coconut
⅔ cup sesame seeds
½ cup sunflower seeds
½ cup bran flakes
1 cup nuts, such as almonds, pecans, or hazelnuts, coarsely chopped

Preheat the oven to 275°F. Lightly grease a shallow roasting pan. In a small saucepan over medium heat, combine the oil, honey, vanilla and almond extracts, and water. Heat until well combined, and set aside. In a large bowl, mix together the oats, wheat germ, coconut, sesame seeds, sunflower seeds, bran flakes, and nuts. Pour the honey mixture over the dry ingredients. Mix well to thoroughly combine; mixing with your hands works best. Transfer to the prepared roasting pan. Bake, uncovered, for about 90 minutes, stirring every 15 minutes to prevent burning. Bake until completely dry and golden brown. Allow to cool completely. Store in an airtight container.

Spiced Honey Corn Grits

This comforting, richly aromatic cereal is a favorite in the fall when the crisp air has turned the tundra into a tapestry of reds and golds.

Yield: 6 cups cooked cereal

4 cups whole milk
2 tablespoons butter
½ cup honey
2 tablespoons vanilla extract
1 tablespoon ground cinnamon
1 tablespoon ground ginger
1 teaspoon ground cloves
¼ teaspoon ground mace
¼ teaspoon ground nutmeg
⅛ teaspoon salt
1½ cups corn grits
Honey for garnish

In a large, heavy-bottomed saucepan, combine the milk, butter, honey, vanilla, cinnamon, ginger, cloves, mace, nutmeg, and salt. Bring to a boil over medium-high heat. Reduce the heat and stir in the corn grits very slowly. Keep stirring until all the grits are incorporated. Cover and cook over low heat for 30 minutes, stirring frequently to avoid any lumps. Adjust the seasonings. Serve with a swirl of honey on top.

Breakfast Entrées

We love to share Denali National Park with all our guests. Whether we'll be scaling steep mountain slopes, hiking a remote valley, or learning about Denali's flora and fauna, we begin the day's adventure with a wholesome, hearty, delicious breakfast.

Egg Soufflé with Mild Green Chiles

Serve this soufflé with Cornmeal Drop Scones (see page 33) and fresh Citrus Salsa for a wonderfully simple, delicious brunch.

Yield: 10 to 12 servings

10 eggs
½ cup all-purpose flour
1 teaspoon baking powder
¼ teaspoon salt
2 cups cottage cheese
1 pound Monterey Jack cheese, grated
1 (8-ounce) can diced green chiles (found in the Mexican foods section
   of most grocery stores)

Preheat the oven to 350°F. Lightly butter a 9-by-13-inch casserole dish, and set aside. Whisk the eggs until light and fluffy. Gently fold in the flour, baking powder, salt, cheeses, and chiles. Pour into the prepared dish. Bake, uncovered, for 35 minutes. The top should be golden brown and the center should be set. Allow to cool for 10 minutes before serving.

Citrus Salsa

Yield: 2½ to 3 cups, depending on the size of the fruit

2 blood oranges
2 navel oranges
2 tangerines
1 pink grapefruit
2 tablespoons sugar
½ cup fresh chopped cilantro
Pan spray

Preheat oven to 425°F. Using a serrated knife, cut the rinds and pith away from the blood and navel oranges, tangerines, and grapefruit. Slice the fruit through the center, forming rounds. Spray a sheet pan with pan spray. Arrange the fruit in a single layer on the pan. Sprinkle the sugar over the top of the fruit. Bake in oven 10 minutes until sugar has caramelized. Allow to cool slightly. Coarsely chop the fruit. Mix together with the chopped cilantro. Serve with Egg Soufflé with Mild Green Chiles.

Swedish Oven Pancake

This Camp Denali breakfast tradition is very much like a large, sweet popover. We bring it to the table in large cast iron skillets and serve it with our own Alaskan Lingonberry Syrup (see page 30).

Yield: 8 servings

2 tablespoons solid vegetable shortening
2 cups all-purpose flour
¼ cup sugar
1 teaspoon salt
6 eggs
4 cups whole milk

Preheat the oven to 450°F. Measure the shortening into a large cast iron skillet and preheat the skillet in the oven.

In a medium bowl, mix together the flour, sugar, and salt. In a separate bowl, whisk the eggs until light and fluffy. Slowly pour some of the milk into the dry ingredients. Mix well until lump free. Continue adding the milk, mixing to avoid lumps. Gently fold in the eggs. Carefully remove the skillet from the oven. Swirl the skillet carefully to coat it with hot shortening. Pour the batter into the skillet (the batter should sizzle). Return the skillet to the oven and bake for 15 minutes. Reduce the temperature to 375°F and continue to bake, without opening the oven, for 20 minutes more. Carefully remove the skillet from the oven. The pancake should be golden brown and very puffy. Serve immediately with the toppings of your choice.

SOURDOUGH

Sourdough is a frontier tradition. Early pioneers relied on their perpetual sourdough sponge for leavening pancakes, biscuits, and breads.

Sourdough Starter

Original starters may have owed their particular flavor to wild yeasts captured from the air when a mixture of flour and water was allowed to ferment over a couple of days. Here is the recipe for a speedier version.

Yield: 2 cups starter

2 cups warm water
1 tablespoon active dry yeast
2 cups all-purpose flour

In a bowl, measure the warm water, add the yeast, and allow it to dissolve. Mix in the flour, a little at a time. When well mixed, transfer the starter to a ceramic crock. Loosely cover the crock; a plate will do. Allow it to rest at room temperature for 48 hours prior to use.

To replenish the starter, add equal parts water and flour. Once you have the starter, you can keep it going indefinitely. You can store your starter in the refrigerator; just allow it to come to room temperature before using. If any liquid rises to the top of your starter, stir it back in.

We had these on 3rd morning.

Sourdough Pancakes

We serve these with our own Alaskan Blueberry Syrup (see page 30) and maple syrup from the Cole family farm in Maine.

Yield: 8 servings, 16 4-inch pancakes

⅓ cup warm water
1½ cups Sourdough Starter (see previous recipe)
1¼ cups buttermilk
3½ cups all-purpose flour
4 eggs, separated
2½ tablespoons vegetable oil
2½ tablespoons honey
⅛ teaspoon salt
1 teaspoon baking soda

In a large bowl, mix together the water and sourdough starter. Mix in the buttermilk and flour. Transfer to a large stainless steel container. Cover loosely and keep in a warm place overnight.

In the morning, whisk the egg whites until they hold stiff peaks. In a separate bowl, combine the egg yolks, oil, honey, and salt. Fold into the sourdough mixture. Gently fold in the egg whites, and then fold in the baking soda.

Preheat a frying pan over medium-high heat. Lightly butter the pan. Using a ¼-cup measure, pour dollops of batter into the pan. Adjust the heat and cook until tiny air bubbles appear on the surface, then gently flip the pancake. Continue cooking until evenly colored on both sides. Stack the pancakes loosely, covered with foil, while you cook the remaining batter. Serve immediately with your favorite toppings.

Quiche

Quiche can be made ahead, so it works perfectly for brunch. It also freezes well. Be sure it is completely thawed before reheating.

Quiche Crust

The substitution of milk for water makes this dough very easy to work and produces a tender crumb. The recipe makes four crusts that you can also use for any pie or tart.

Yield: 4 single 9- to 10-inch pie crusts

5 cups all-purpose flour
2 teaspoons salt
1 pound (4 sticks) unsalted butter, cubed and chilled
About ½ cup whole milk (you may need a little more or less)

In the bowl of an electric mixer fitted with the whisk attachment, measure the flour, salt, and butter. Whisk until the butter is cut into the flour; the mixture should resemble crumbs and pebbles. Change to the paddle attachment. With the mixer on the lowest speed, dribble in the milk. Continue adding milk just until the dough comes together; this should happen very fast. Divide the dough into 4 pieces, and flatten each into a disk. Wrap in plastic and refrigerate or freeze. The dough needs to relax and chill prior to use.

2ⁿᵈ morning with red peppers, onion & zucchini # Quiche

Quiche can be made with most any kind of cheese and a variety of fillings. Sautéed vegetables, sliced tomatoes with basil, sautéed wild mushrooms, wilted spinach with golden raisins, smoked salmon and dill, Lorraine (cooked bacon and parsley), sautéed chopped leeks, and cooked chicken are just a few of the possibilities.

Yield: One 10-inch quiche

Quiche Crust for 1 pie shell (see previous recipe)
1½ cups heavy cream
4 eggs
⅛ teaspoon ground nutmeg
⅛ teaspoon ground white pepper
⅛ teaspoon salt
Filling of your choice (see ideas above or invent your own)
2 cups grated cheese (any kind)

Preheat the oven to 350°F. On a lightly floured surface, roll out the dough. Transfer to a 10-inch pie pan, and overlay it with foil and baking weights (uncooked beans work well as weights). Bake for 15 minutes, then remove weights and foil. Continue baking for 10 minutes more.

In a medium bowl, whisk the cream, eggs, nutmeg, pepper, and salt until well combined. Line the crust with the filling of your choice. Top with the grated cheese. Carefully pour the egg mixture over the filling and cheese. It should come almost to the top of the shell. Return to the oven and bake for 30 to 40 minutes, until the center is set and the top is golden brown. Let cool for 10 minutes before cutting.

Frittata

This frittata is tasty and easy to prepare. It's also a great use for day-old bread.

Yield: 8 to 10 servings

5 large red bell peppers, roasted, peeled, and seeded
5 eggs
1½ cups heavy cream
⅛ teaspoon salt
⅛ teaspoon ground white pepper
⅛ teaspoon ground nutmeg
1 loaf day-old bread, thickly sliced and slightly dried
1 bunch asparagus, trimmed and lightly sautéed
2 cups grated Swiss cheese
1 cup grated Parmesan cheese
1 bunch parsley, chopped

Chop or slice the roasted red peppers. Mix together the eggs, cream, salt, pepper, and nutmeg. Set aside. Preheat the oven to 375°F. Lightly butter a casserole dish. Arrange the bread, asparagus, and peppers in the dish, interspersed with some of the Swiss and Parmesan cheeses. Top with the remaining cheese, and sprinkle with parsley. Pour the reserved egg mixture over all. Cover loosely with aluminum foil. Bake for 45 minutes. Remove the foil, and bake for an additional 15 minutes, until the top is puffy and golden and the center is set. Allow to cool for 10 minutes before serving. Cut into squares to serve.

Hazelnut-Crusted French Toast

This is an elegant way to serve French Toast. For a tropical-inspired dish, omit the spices and substitute 1 cup chopped macadamia nuts mixed with 1 cup shredded coconut for the hazelnuts.

Yield: 10 slices

4 eggs
1 cup whole milk
¼ cup heavy cream
1 teaspoon vanilla extract
1 teaspoon almond extract
1 teaspoon ground cinnamon
¼ teaspoon ground cloves
¼ teaspoon ground nutmeg
2 cups coarsely chopped hazelnuts
10 thick slices day-old French bread

Preheat the oven to 425°F. (The oven needs to be at a true 400°F when the French Toast goes in. Ovens lose a huge amount of heat when the door is opened. For this recipe it is important that the French Toast cooks quickly, keeping the interior moist while toasting the nuts.) Grease a sheet pan with margarine, or spray with nonstick cooking spray. *Do not use butter; it will burn.* In a wide, shallow bowl or pie plate, mix the eggs, milk, cream, vanilla extract, almond extract, cinnamon, cloves, and nutmeg. Place the nuts on a plate. Set 4 slices of bread in the bowl. Allow to sit for a few seconds to saturate the bread. Turn the bread to coat it completely. Dredge the soaked bread in the chopped nuts. Set the soaked bread on the sheet pan and repeat with the remaining bread.

Reduce the oven temperature to 400°F. Bake for 10 minutes. Flip the bread and bake for 10 minutes more. Remove from the oven. The nuts should look toasted, and the bread should be cooked all the way through. Serve with your favorite toppings.

Breakfast Breads

The bakery at Camp Denali provides tender tasty treats for both of our lodges. Early in the morning the breakfast breads are fetched from the bakery and delivered to the cooks to finish off in the ovens right before the bell announces breakfast. These breads go right from the oven to our guests. No breakfast is complete without a delicious sweet bread fresh from our bakery.

Mix-It-In Muffins

You will become a muffin master with this recipe.

Yield: 12 large muffins or 18 standard-size muffins

3 cups all-purpose flour
⅔ cup sugar
1 tablespoon baking powder
½ teaspoon baking soda
½ teaspoon salt
½ pound (2 sticks) butter, melted
2 cups sour cream (you can substitute 1 cup sour cream with 1 cup yogurt)
2 large eggs
2 teaspoons vanilla extract
2 cups fresh or frozen fruit, such as blueberries, raspberries, or diced peaches
1½ cups Streusel Topping (optional; recipe follows)

Preheat the oven to 375°F. Butter muffin tins. In a large bowl, combine the flour, sugar, baking powder, baking soda, and salt. In a separate bowl, combine the butter, sour cream, eggs, and vanilla. Mix the wet ingredients into the dry ingredients very gently, just until the dough comes together. Fold in the fruit. (If you're using frozen fruit, first toss it in a bit of flour.) Fill the muffin tins two-thirds full. Sprinkle the tops with Streusel Topping, if desired. Bake for 30 minutes. Using a toothpick, make sure the center is set. Allow to cool for 5 minutes in the pan. Remove from the pan and cool completely.

Streusel Topping for Muffins and Coffee Cakes

Make a double batch of this topping and freeze some to use later. You can take it right from the freezer; there is no need to defrost it prior to use.

Yield: 3 cups, enough for 2 batches of muffins or 2 coffee cakes

1⅔ cups powdered sugar
1⅓ cups all-purpose flour
3 tablespoons ground cinnamon
12 tablespoons butter, cubed

In the bowl of an electric mixer fitted with the paddle attachment, combine all ingredients. Mix until light and fluffy, with a crumblike texture. Sprinkle on top of muffins or coffee cakes.

Cinnamon Pull-Aparts

These sticky, pull-apart cinnamon rolls are made with a yeast dough that needs time to rise. You can prepare the dough the night before, let it rise, and refrigerate it. The next morning, allow it to warm to room temperature before forming the pull-aparts.

Yield: 20 pull-aparts

Dough
1 cup warm water
¼ cup sugar
2 teaspoons active dry yeast
3½ cups all-purpose flour, divided
¼ cup powdered milk
4 tablespoons butter, softened
1 egg
1 teaspoon salt

Sauce for Bottom of Pan(s)
5 tablespoons butter, melted
⅓ cup brown sugar
½ cup chopped pecans

Coating for Pull-Aparts
½ cup white sugar
¼ cup brown sugar
1½ tablespoons ground cinnamon
¼ teaspoon ground allspice
¼ teaspoon ground nutmeg
8 tablespoons butter (1 stick), melted

To make the dough: In a large bowl, combine the warm water with the sugar, and sprinkle the yeast on top. Allow the yeast to dissolve and become frothy. Stir in 1 cup of the flour and all the powdered milk. Mix until well combined, then add the butter, egg, and salt. Mix well. Incorporate the rest of the flour until a soft dough is formed. Turn out into a buttered bowl, cover, and let rise until doubled in volume and gently punch down dough. At this point you can refrigerate the dough overnight or proceed with the recipe.

To prepare the pan(s): Pour the melted butter into a 10-inch tube or Bundt pan or 2 loaf pans. Sprinkle the brown sugar over the butter, and top with the chopped nuts.

To coat the pull-aparts: Divide the dough into 20 pieces. In a small bowl, combine the white sugar, brown sugar, cinnamon, allspice, and nutmeg. Dip each hunk of dough into the melted butter, then dredge lightly in the sugar mixture. Place the coated hunks in a single layer in the prepared pan or pans. Cover and let rise until almost doubled.

To bake: Preheat the oven to 350°F. Set the pans on a parchment-lined sheet pan, and bake for 45 minutes. Allow to cool in the pan for 5 minutes. Invert the pan onto a serving plate or platter, and leave the pan on top of the pull-aparts to cool for a few more minutes. Remove the pan and serve.

2nd morning

Citrus Scones

These scones are a taste of sunshine.

Yield: 12 scones

7 tablespoons butter
2½ cups all-purpose flour
¼ cup sugar
¼ teaspoon baking soda
1 tablespoon baking powder
1 teaspoon salt
2 eggs
¼ cup whole milk
¼ cup buttermilk
¼ cup sour cream
¼ cup grated orange zest
½ to 1 cup Orange Glaze (recipe follows)

Preheat the oven to 375°F. Cut the butter into small cubes and chill. In a large bowl, combine the flour, sugar, baking soda, baking powder, and salt. In a separate bowl, combine the eggs, milk, buttermilk, and sour cream. Cut the butter into the flour mixture until the mixture resembles coarse crumbs. Gently mix in the milk mixture. Fold in the orange zest. Mix just until the dough comes together. Turn out on to a lightly floured surface. Gently roll the dough out to the desired thickness and cut it into the desired shapes. Place on a sheet pan lined with parchment paper and bake for 15 to 20 minutes, until golden brown. Remove from the oven and allow to cool slightly. Brush with Orange Glaze and serve.

Orange Glaze

Yield: 1 cup

1 cup powdered sugar
2 tablespoons orange juice concentrate
2 tablespoons freshly squeezed orange juice

Mix together all ingredients. Add more powdered sugar or orange juice as necessary to adjust the consistency. Brush over the tops of slightly cooled scones.

Blueberry Syrup

served with sourdough pancakes

Yield: 1 gallon

1 gallon blueberries
8 cups sugar
1½ cups apple juice

Measure the berries, sugar, and apple juice into a large blender and process until well mashed. Pour into a large, heavy-bottomed stock pot. Slowly bring to a boil, adding more juice if needed. Cook for 20 minutes at a hard, rolling boil. Ladle into hot, sterilized jars and seal with sterilized lids. Allow to cool before moving.

Lingonberry Sauce

Yield: 1 gallon

1 gallon lingonberries
10 cups sugar
2 cups apple juice

Mix together lingonberries, sugar, and juice in a large, heavy-bottomed stock pot. Boil for 20 minutes, being careful not to burn. Ladle into hot, sterilized jars and seal with sterilized lids. Allow to cool before moving.

1ˢᵗ morning

Lingonberry Braid

Every fall, in the hills surrounding Camp Denali and North Face Lodge, we gather gallons and gallons of fresh lingonberries to make our own syrup and jam. We make our Lingonberry Sauce tart and thick. The lovely ruby red of the sauce against the golden brown bread in the braid makes this a festive addition to any holiday brunch.

Yield: 2 braids

Dough
1 cup warm water
⅓ cup sugar
2 teaspoons active dry yeast
2½ cups all-purpose flour, divided
¼ cup powdered milk
6 tablespoons butter, softened
2 eggs
½ teaspoon salt

Filling
½ cup almond paste
2 tablespoons blanched almonds
1 egg
2 cups Lingonberry Sauce (if not available, use cranberry sauce)

Egg Wash
1 egg
1½ tablespoons water

Powdered sugar, for dusting

To make the dough: In a large bowl, combine the warm water with the sugar, and sprinkle the yeast on top. Allow the yeast to dissolve and become frothy. Stir in 1 cup of the flour and all the powdered milk. Mix until well combined, then add the butter, eggs, and salt. Mix well. Add the rest of the flour until a soft dough is formed. Turn out into a buttered bowl and let rise until doubled in volume.

To make the almond filling: Using a food processor, combine the almond paste, almonds, and egg. Purée until a thick paste is formed.

To assemble and bake the braids: Preheat the oven to 375°F. Punch the dough down and divide it in half. Roll out one piece to a 12-by-6-inch rectangle, about ¼ inch thick. Without cutting the dough, divide it into thirds lengthwise by making 2 lengthwise indentations in the dough. In the center third, spread half of the almond mixture, and top it with 1 cup of the Lingonberry Sauce. On the outer thirds, cut 12 equal diagonal slits, 1 inch deep, from the edges toward the center. Fold these in overlapping rows over the center filling, pinching the ends to seal. Repeat with the remaining dough and filling.

Cover and let rise in a warm place until almost doubled, about 45 minutes. Mix the egg and water together to make an egg wash. Gently brush the braids with the egg wash. Bake for 30 minutes. Remove from the oven and cool. Dust with powdered sugar and serve.

Cornmeal Drop Scones

Yield: 12 scones

1¾ cups cake flour
¾ cup cornmeal
¼ teaspoon baking soda
1 tablespoon baking powder
1 teaspoon salt
1 teaspoon cinnamon
6 tablespoons butter, melted
¼ cup buttermilk
¼ cup sour cream
½ cup honey
2 eggs
1 tablespoon vanilla
2 tablespoons milk

For the glaze
3 tablespoons sweetened condensed milk
1 egg white

Preheat oven to 375°F. In a large bowl combine the flour, cornmeal, baking soda, baking powder, salt, and cinnamon. In a separate bowl combine the butter, buttermilk, sour cream, and honey. Using a wooden spoon or a sturdy rubber spatula, mix the wet ingredients into the dry ingredients. Gently mix, adding more milk if needed to form a soft doughy batter. Using an ice cream scoop or large serving spoon, scoop/drop the scones onto a sheet pan lined with parchment paper. In a small bowl, whisk together the sweetened condensed milk and the egg white. Brush this on the tops of the scones. Bake for 15 to 20 minutes. Scones should be golden brown and lift off the pan easily.

Cool slightly before serving.

Cream Cheese Muffins

These muffins freeze very well.

Yield: 12 muffins

1 cup (8 ounces) cream cheese
2 eggs
1 cup sugar
½ cup vegetable oil
2 teaspoons vanilla extract
2 cups all-purpose flour
½ teaspoon salt
½ teaspoon baking soda
1 teaspoon baking powder
1 cup crushed berries (fresh or frozen)

Preheat the oven to 375°F. Grease 12 muffin tins. In an electric mixer fitted with the paddle attachment, beat the cream cheese until completely smooth. With the mixer on low speed, add the eggs, one at a time. Add the sugar, vegetable oil, and vanilla. In a separate bowl, combine the flour, salt, baking soda, and baking powder. Slowly incorporate the dry ingredients into the cream cheese mixture. Fold in the berries. Scoop into the prepared muffin tins. Bake for 20 to 25 minutes. The tops should be golden brown. Use a toothpick to make sure the center is set. Allow to cool in the tins for 10 minutes. Remove from the tins and cool to room temperature. Serve.

Lemon Cream Scones

Try these with strawberry jam.

Yield: 12 scones

Scones
2 cups all-purpose flour
⅓ cup sugar
1 tablespoon baking powder
¼ teaspoon salt
¾ cup chopped fresh apricots
1 tablespoon grated lemon zest
1¼ cups heavy cream

Topping
1 tablespoon grated lemon zest
2 tablespoons sugar
3 tablespoons butter, melted

To make the scones: Preheat the oven to 375°F. In a large bowl, combine the flour, sugar, baking powder, and salt. Add the apricots and lemon zest, and mix well. Slowly add the cream, mixing just until a dough forms. Turn out onto a lightly floured surface, roll out to the desired thickness, and cut into the desired shapes. Transfer to a sheet pan lined with parchment paper.

To make the topping: Mix together the lemon zest and sugar. Brush the tops of the scones with melted butter. Sprinkle the lemon sugar over the scones.

Bake for 15 to 20 minutes. The scones will be light golden brown. Serve warm.

Blueberry Almond Coffee Cake

Fresh, tart Alaskan blueberries make this coffee cake very special. Wild berries work best, but you can substitute any type of berry you prefer.

Yield: One 9-inch cake

Cake
¼ pound (1 stick) butter, softened
1¼ cups sugar
2 eggs
1 teaspoon vanilla extract
1 teaspoon almond extract
2 cups all-purpose flour
2 teaspoons baking powder
¾ teaspoon salt
½ cup whole milk
2 cups blueberries

Meringue Topping
3 egg whites
3 tablespoons sugar
1 cup sliced almonds

To make the cake: Preheat the oven to 350°F. Butter a 9-inch springform pan. Line the bottom of the pan with parchment paper. Using an electric mixer fitted with the paddle attachment, beat the butter and sugar until light and fluffy. With the mixer on low speed, add the eggs, one at a time, and beat until light and fluffy. Slowly add the vanilla and almond extracts. In a separate bowl, combine the flour, baking powder, and salt. Slowly add the flour mixture to the butter and egg mixture, alternating with the milk. Scrape down the sides of the bowl. Mix well until the batter is smooth. Fold in the blueberries. Pour the batter into the prepared pan.

To make the topping: In a clean bowl, whisk the egg whites to soft peaks, add the sugar, and beat until stiff peaks form. Fold in the almonds. Spoon the meringue mixture on top of the batter.

Bake the cake for 1 hour. Using a toothpick, check the center of the cake for doneness. The tester will come out clean when done. Allow to cool in the pan for 10 minutes. Remove from the pan and allow to cool for another 10 minutes before cutting. Serve warm.

Lunch

Our first priority is to share with our guests some of the splendor and awe of this great national park. Whether they're participating in a naturalist-guided field trip into the backcountry or an independent day with book, bike, or canoe, our make-it-yourself lunch buffet becomes the sustenance for the day's outings. Many people have savored the following offerings while resting on a wildflower-strewn ridgetop, with a grizzly family foraging below the icy white backdrop of North America's highest mountain. Although the recipes in this chapter were created with a picnic in mind, they all work great served at home or in the office.

Sandwich Breads

Both of the breads that follow use a flour that is high in gluten. Gluten helps to develop the integrity of the bread and is the secret to great crumb and texture. You can find gluten flour at health food stores, or substitute bread flour for the all-purpose flour.

Dill Rye Bread

This bread tastes especially wonderful when served with smoked Alaskan halibut or salmon.

Yield: Two 1-pound loaves

1½ cups warm water
1 cup Sourdough Starter (see page 19)
2 tablespoons honey
2 tablespoons molasses
1 tablespoon active dry yeast
¼ cup pure gluten flour
1½ cups rye flour
4½ cups all-purpose flour
2 tablespoons dried onion
1 tablespoon dried dill weed
1 teaspoon dill seeds
1 tablespoon salt
¼ cup olive oil
1 tablespoon butter, melted

In the bowl of an electric mixer, combine the water, Sourdough Starter, honey, and molasses. Using a rubber spatula, mix in the yeast. Allow the yeast to dissolve and become frothy.

In a separate bowl, combine the gluten flour, rye flour, all-purpose flour, onion, dill weed, dill seeds, and salt. With a rubber spatula, mix half of the flour mixture into the yeast mixture. Using the dough hook attachment, slowly incorporate the remaining flour mixture, alternating with the olive oil. Continue to add flour until the dough is smooth, soft, and elastic.

Turn the dough out into an oiled bowl, turning it to oil the top. Cover loosely and let rise in a warm place until almost doubled in volume. Gently punch down the dough and turn out onto a lightly floured work surface. Divide the dough in half. Knead and shape it into oblong loaves. Place on a lightly buttered sheet pan. Cover loosely and let rise in a warm place until almost doubled in volume.

Preheat the oven to 375°F. Brush the tops of the loaves with the melted butter. Gently slash the tops of the loaves diagonally, making 3 cuts, ¼ inch deep, per loaf. Bake at 375°F for 20 minutes. Reduce the heat to 325°F and continue to bake for an additional 20 to 25 minutes. Remove from the oven and remove from the pan. Cool completely on a cooling rack before slicing.

Basic Sandwich Bread

Create new variations by adding dried fruit, leftover hot cereal, mashed potatoes, or sourdough starter.

Yield: Two 1¾-pound loaves

2 cups warm water
¼ cup honey
1 tablespoon active dry yeast
3 cups all-purpose flour, divided
⅓ cup powdered milk
2 cups whole wheat flour
¼ cup gluten flour
2 tablespoons butter, softened
1 tablespoon salt

In the bowl of an electric mixer, combine the water, honey, and yeast. Mix with a rubber spatula, and allow the yeast to dissolve and become frothy. Using a rubber spatula, mix in 2 cups of the all-purpose flour. Using the dough hook attachment with the mixer on low speed, add the powdered milk, whole wheat flour, and gluten flour. Mix well until the consistency is smooth. Add the butter and salt, and mix well. Slowly incorporate the remaining flour. Continue adding flour until the dough is elastic and smooth. It should pull away from the inside of the bowl.

Turn the dough out into an oiled bowl, turning it to oil the top. Cover loosely and let rise in a warm place until almost doubled in volume.

Gently punch down the dough. Transfer to a lightly floured work surface. Cut the dough in half. Knead the halves into smooth rounds. Roll each piece out ½-inch thick, the length of a loaf pan. Lightly butter 2 loaf pans. Roll the dough up into an oblong shape. Pinch the seam smooth. Set the loaves, seam side down, in the pans. Cover loosely and let rise in a warm place until almost doubled in volume.

Preheat the oven to 350°F. Gently slash the tops of the loaves, making cuts ¼-inch deep. Bake for 45 to 55 minutes. Remove from the oven and remove from the pans. Cool completely on racks before slicing.

Sandwich Spreads and Salads

Included in our buffet of luncheon meats, cheeses, and fresh greenhouse greens is always a delicious variety of sandwich spreads and salads.

Chicken Salad with Almonds and Grapes

This salad is especially wonderful on toasted Honey Curry Bread (see page 124).

Yield: 6 servings

3 boneless, skinless chicken breasts, cooked and chopped
2 tablespoons Dijon mustard
½ cup mayonnaise
⅓ cup minced red onion
½ cup diced celery
Salt and freshly ground pepper
½ cup chopped fresh cilantro
½ cup sliced almonds, toasted
1½ cups red seedless grapes, halved

In a large bowl, combine the chicken, mustard, mayonnaise, onion, celery, and salt and pepper to taste. Stir to coat all ingredients evenly. Mix in the cilantro and almonds. Fold in the grapes. Refrigerate for ½ hour to combine the flavors.

Smoked Halibut Salad, Béarnaise Style

You can substitute cooked fresh halibut for the smoked halibut.

Yield: 6 servings

2 tablespoons Dijon mustard
½ cup mayonnaise
½ cup diced celery
⅓ cup minced shallots
2 tablespoons grated orange zest
⅓ cup chopped fresh tarragon
3 cups flaked smoked halibut
½ cup pine nuts, toasted
Salt and freshly ground pepper

In a large bowl, combine the mustard, mayonnaise, celery, shallots, orange zest, and tarragon. Mix well. Fold in the halibut and pine nuts. Season to taste with salt and pepper. Taste and adjust the seasonings. Refrigerate for ½ hour to combine the flavors.

White Bean Pesto Spread

Serve with crostini for a great vegetarian appetizer.

Yield: 2 cups

2 cups basil leaves
2 teaspoons crushed garlic
¼ cup grated Parmesan cheese
¼ cup pine nuts, toasted
1 cup olive oil, divided
1 teaspoon kosher salt
1 teaspoon freshly ground pepper
2 cups cooked white beans, drained and rinsed twice

In the bowl of a food processor, purée the basil, garlic, cheese, and pine nuts. Slowly add ½ cup of the olive oil while the food processor is running. Add the salt and pepper. Add the white beans and continue adding the remaining oil until the mixture is the correct consistency. Taste and adjust the seasonings.

Tuna Niçoise Salad

Try this salad on a bed of pasta for dinner.

Yield: 4 cups

2 tablespoons red wine vinegar
2 teaspoons sugar
1 tablespoon fresh lemon juice
1 teaspoon minced garlic
1 tablespoon Dijon mustard
½ cup mayonnaise
1 tablespoon chopped fresh thyme
1 tablespoon chopped fresh oregano
2 tablespoons chiffonade (thin strips) of fresh basil
⅓ cup pitted, halved kalamata olives
½ cup minced sun-dried tomatoes
4 (6-ounce) cans tuna, well drained and flaked
Salt and freshly ground pepper

In a small bowl, mix together the red wine vinegar, sugar, lemon juice, garlic, and mustard. Whisk until well combined, and then whisk in the mayonnaise.

Fold in the thyme, oregano, basil, olives, and tomatoes. Mix in the tuna. Season to taste with salt and pepper and adjust the other seasonings.

Hummus

This Middle Eastern specialty makes a great appetizer platter when served with pita toast points, cucumber, fresh tomatoes, and feta cheese. Use this recipe as a base, creating different flavors by adding any herbs and seasonings you prefer. One of our favorite additions is roasted red peppers.

Yield: 4 cups

3 cups cooked garbanzo beans (about 1 cup raw garbanzo beans,
   cooked, or 2 cans, 16 ounces each, drained)
¼ cup fresh lemon juice
2 teaspoons crushed garlic
3 tablespoons sesame oil
3 tablespoons olive oil
½ cup chopped fresh parsley
Salt and freshly ground pepper

In a food processor, purée all ingredients until smooth. If the mixture is too thick, add a little more lemon juice and olive oil. Taste and adjust the seasonings. Refrigerate for ½ hour to combine the flavors.

Southwestern Kippered Salmon Salad

This salad has quite a kick to it. If you prefer a milder dish, omit the adobo sauce. Try serving it wrapped in a tortilla for a quick sandwich on the go. Adobo sauce can be found in the Mexican foods section of most supermarkets. You can freeze any sauce you have left over, or store it in the refrigerator. It will keep for a few weeks.

Yield: 4 cups

1 cup sour cream
1 teaspoon adobo sauce
2 cups flaked kippered salmon
½ cup peeled, seeded, diced cucumber
¼ cup diced red bell pepper
¼ cup minced red onion
⅓ cup chopped fresh cilantro
2 teaspoons chili powder
2 teaspoons ground cumin
Salt

In a small bowl, combine the sour cream and adobo sauce; set aside. In a large bowl combine the salmon, cucumber, pepper, onion, cilantro, chili powder, cumin, and salt. Mix well, and then add in the sour cream mixture. Taste and adjust the seasonings. Serve immediately.

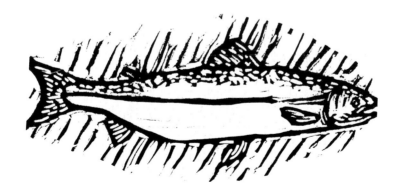

Picnic Pasta Salad

Traditionally served at our picnic en route to Camp Denali and North Face Lodge, this pasta salad can be made well in advance. If the pasta absorbs all of the dressing, toss it with about 3 tablespoons of warm water.

Yield: 10 servings

5 cups pasta spirals
4 tablespoons olive oil
½ cup mayonnaise
¾ cup yogurt
¼ cup dill pickle juice
¾ cup chopped fresh herbs, such as basil, dill, and chives
1 tablespoon dried dill weed
¾ cup chopped fresh parsley
1 teaspoon crushed garlic, pressed with a garlic press or a mortar and pestle
1 teaspoon kosher salt
1 teaspoon lemon pepper
1 teaspoon freshly ground black pepper
10 kalamata olives, sliced
¼ cup diced dill pickles
½ large red onion, julienned
1 cup diced Roma tomatoes
½ cup diced artichoke hearts
½ cup diced zucchini
½ cup diced summer squash

In a large pot of boiling, salted water, cook the pasta until tender, approximately 12 minutes. In a large colander, drain the pasta, rinse under cold water, and drain again. Toss the pasta with 4 tablespoons of olive oil, and set aside. In a large bowl, combine the mayonnaise, yogurt, pickle juice, dill, parsley, garlic, salt, lemon pepper, and black pepper. Gently toss the pasta in the dressing. Gently stir in the olives, pickles, onion, tomatoes, artichokes, zucchini, and squash. Refrigerate for at least ½ hour to combine the flavors.

Homemade Mayonnaise

Although purchased mayonnaise is a typical condiment for most households, nothing beats the flavor of homemade.

Yield: 2 cups

4 egg yolks
2 teaspoons kosher salt
1⅔ cups olive oil
1 tablespoon fresh lemon juice
Cayenne pepper

In a small bowl, whisk the egg yolks and salt together until light and fluffy. Slowly add the oil, drop by drop, whisking rapidly. When half of the oil is incorporated, whisk in the lemon juice. Continue whisking and adding oil until the mayonnaise is the desired consistency. Season to taste with cayenne pepper. Refrigerate for up to 1 week.

Gorp

Gorp is a snack mix that provides the energy surge the body needs on a long day hike. Although there are as many versions of this snack as there are people who eat it, here are two of our favorites.

Candy Gorp

Yield: 14 cups

1 cup hazelnuts, toasted
1 cup peanuts, toasted
1 cup almonds, toasted
½ cup walnuts, toasted
½ cup dry-roasted sunflower seeds
1 cup unsweetened flaked coconut
2 cups raisins
1 cup date pieces
1 cup dried papaya pieces
1 cup banana chips
4 cups M&M's

Combine all ingredients, mixing thoroughly. Store in an airtight container.

Chex Gorp

Yield: 16 cups

½ cup margarine
2 tablespoons butter
3 tablespoons soy sauce
2 teaspoons garlic powder
½ teaspoon cayenne
9 cups Corn Chex or Rice Chex cereal
1½ cups almonds, toasted
1 cup hulled pumpkin seeds, toasted
1 cup dry-roasted sunflower seeds
2 cups Chinese-style crisp noodles (chow mein noodles)
2 cups small, crisp pretzels

Preheat the oven to 275°F. In a small pan over medium heat, melt together the margarine and butter. Add the soy sauce, garlic powder, and cayenne. Cook over low heat for 5 minutes.

In a large bowl, combine the cereal, almonds, pumpkin and sunflower seeds, and crisp noodles. Pour the butter mixture over the cereal mixture. Mix well, completely coating the cereal mixture. Turn out onto a large, shallow roasting pan. Bake until the cereal is very dry and golden, stirring every 15 minutes to avoid burning. This should take about 1 hour. Remove from the oven and cool completely. When cool, stir in the pretzels. Store in an airtight container.

Cookies and Bars

Although fresh fruit is always available, it seems to take second place to these cookies, cupcakes, and brownies.

Chocolate Cream Cheese Cupcakes

Making a double batch of these is always a safe bet. They seem to disappear from the pan as they are cooling!

Yield: 12 cupcakes

1 cup (8 ounces) cream cheese
1⅓ cups sugar
1 egg
1 cup semisweet chocolate chips
1½ cups all-purpose flour
1 teaspoon baking soda
¼ cup unsweetened cocoa powder
¾ teaspoon salt
⅓ cup vegetable oil
1 teaspoon cider vinegar
1 teaspoon vanilla extract
¾ cup water

Preheat the oven to 300°F. Line muffin tins with cupcake liners. Using an electric mixer fitted with a paddle attachment, beat together on high speed the cream cheese and sugar until light and fluffy. Reduce the speed, and mix in the egg. Continue to beat until light and fluffy. Fold in the chocolate chips and set aside.

In a separate bowl, combine the flour, baking soda, cocoa, and salt. In a third bowl, combine the oil, cider vinegar, vanilla, and water. Mix the liquid mixture into the flour mixture until smooth.

Fill the prepared muffin tins half full with the dark batter. Top with a dollop of the cream cheese mixture. Bake for 20 to 25 minutes. Cool in the pan for 10 minutes before gently transferring the cupcakes to a cooling rack.

Double Chocolate Brownies

These are a staff favorite. Split one in half and fill it with vanilla ice cream for a taste sensation that is out of this world.

Yield: 20 brownies

4 ounces unsweetened chocolate
½ pound (2 sticks) plus 2⅔ tablespoons butter
4 eggs
2 cups sugar
2 teaspoons vanilla extract
1½ cups all-purpose flour
1 teaspoon baking powder
½ teaspoon salt
½ cup dry-roasted almonds
1 cup semisweet chocolate chips
1 cup mini marshmallows

Preheat the oven to 350°F. Butter well a 9-by-13-inch or similar size baking pan, and set aside. In a small saucepan over low heat, melt together the chocolate and butter; set aside. Using an electric mixer fitted with the whisk attachment, whip the eggs, sugar, and vanilla together until light and fluffy. In a separate bowl, combine the flour, baking powder, and salt. Fold the melted chocolate into the egg mixture. Fold in the flour mixture, and mix until smooth. Fold in the almonds, chocolate chips, and marshmallows. Scrape down the sides of the bowl to incorporate evenly. Pour the batter into the prepared pan. Bake for 30 to 40 minutes. Use a toothpick to make sure the center is cooked. Remove from the oven and cool completely before cutting.

Tangy Lemon Squares

A refreshing, light, and tangy dessert.

Yield: 16 squares

Crust
⅓ cup sugar
3 tablespoons butter, softened
1 cup all-purpose flour

Topping
3 eggs
1 cup white sugar
1 tablespoon grated lemon zest
⅓ cup fresh lemon juice
3 tablespoons all-purpose flour
½ teaspoon baking powder
⅛ teaspoon salt
1 tablespoon powdered sugar

To make the crust: Preheat the oven to 350°F. Grease an 8-inch square baking pan with butter. In an electric mixer fitted with the whisk attachment, whisk together the sugar and butter until light and fluffy. Gradually add the flour. Continue mixing on low speed until the mixture resembles fine crumbs. Gently press the mixture into the prepared pan. Bake for 15 minutes. Allow to cool in the pan on a cooling rack.

To make the topping: In an electric mixer fitted with the whisk attachment, whisk the eggs until light and foamy. Add the sugar, lemon zest, lemon juice, flour, baking powder, and salt. Mix until well incorporated. Pour the mixture into the prepared crust. Return to the oven and bake for 20 to 25 minutes. Test with a toothpick to make sure the middle is set and remove from oven when done. Cool on a cooling rack. Dust the top with powdered sugar. Cut into 16 pieces. Store in an airtight container at room temperature.

Monster Cookies

These delicious cookies should really be in the Camp Denali Classics chapter. We have been making them for as long as I can remember. They are by far the most requested cookie from staff and returning guests. Make them for your family and friends, and you will see how quickly they get gobbled up.

Yield: 2 dozen cookies

¼ pound (1 stick) butter, softened
¾ cup brown sugar
¾ cup white sugar
1 cup peanut butter
3 eggs
1 tablespoon vanilla extract
½ cup all-purpose flour
1 tablespoon baking soda
4 cups rolled oats
½ cup chopped nuts
½ cup M&M's
1 cup semisweet chocolate chips

Preheat the oven to 350°F. Using an electric mixer fitted with the paddle attachment, beat together the butter, brown sugar, white sugar, and peanut butter until light and fluffy. Add the eggs, one at a time, and then add the vanilla. Beat until light and fluffy. In a separate bowl, combine the flour, baking soda, and rolled oats. Gently stir the oats into the butter mixture until well combined. Mix in the nuts, M&M's, and chocolate chips.

Drop tablespoons of dough onto ungreased baking sheets and bake until golden, 10 to 12 minutes. Transfer to a cooling rack to cool.

Glacier Cookies

As this cookie bakes, cracks form in the powdered-sugar crust, causing it to resemble crevasses on a glacier.

Yield: 2½ dozen cookies

3 ounces unsweetened chocolate
¼ pound butter (1 stick), softened
1½ cups white sugar
3 eggs
1 tablespoon vanilla extract
3 cups all-purpose flour
¼ teaspoon salt
2 teaspoons baking powder
⅓ cup whole milk
1 cup powdered sugar

Preheat the oven to 350°F. In a double boiler, melt the chocolate. Remove from the heat and let cool slightly. Using an electric mixer fitted with the paddle attachment, beat together the butter and sugar until light and fluffy.

Add the eggs, one at a time. Beat together until fully incorporated. Add the melted chocolate and the vanilla. Beat until light and fluffy. In a separate bowl, combine the flour, salt, and baking powder. Add the flour mixture to the butter mixture in thirds, alternating with the milk. Mix well.

Use a small ice cream scoop or tablespoon to scoop out balls of dough. Roll in powdered sugar, coating them completely. Set on a sheet pan lined with parchment paper, and bake for 10 to 12 minutes. Allow the cookies to cool in the pan. Store in an airtight container.

Coconut Oatmeal Cookies

Chip coconut gives these cookies wonderful texture and a unique appearance. Chip coconut is large-flake, unsweetened coconut and can be found in bulk at many health food stores. If you have difficulty locating it, substitute with shredded unsweetened coconut. The cookies won't look as unique, but they'll still taste great.

Yield: 3 dozen cookies

3 cups all-purpose flour
1½ teaspoons baking powder
1½ teaspoons baking soda
½ teaspoon salt
⅜ pound (1½ sticks) butter, softened
1¼ cups brown sugar
½ cup white sugar
2 eggs
1 tablespoon vanilla extract
1¼ cups rolled oats
2¼ cups chip coconut

Preheat the oven to 350°F. In a large bowl, combine the flour, baking powder, baking soda, and salt. Using an electric mixer fitted with the paddle attachment, beat together the butter, brown sugar, and white sugar, beating until light and fluffy. Add the eggs one at a time, and then add the vanilla. Beat until light and fluffy. Slowly incorporate the flour mixture until well combined. Mix in the oats and coconut.

Using a tablespoon, scoop out spoonfuls of dough onto baking sheets lined with parchment paper. Bake for 8 to 10 minutes. Cool on pans or cooling racks. Store in an airtight container.

Gingersnaps

The delicate balance of aromatic spices makes these a fragrant, flavorful treat. Spices lose their flavor and potency after time. If the same spices have lined your shelves or drawers for years, it's time to replace them.

Yield: 3 dozen cookies

Cookie Dough
⅜ pound (1½ sticks) butter, softened
½ cup white sugar
⅓ cup brown sugar
¼ cup molasses
1 egg
2¼ cups all-purpose flour
½ tablespoon baking soda
⅛ teaspoon salt
2 teaspoons ground cinnamon
2 teaspoons ground ginger
½ teaspoon ground cloves
½ teaspoon ground allspice

Sugar Coating
1 cup white sugar

Preheat the oven to 350°F. Using an electric mixer fitted with the paddle attachment, beat together the butter, white sugar, and brown sugar until light and fluffy. Slowly incorporate the molasses and egg. Beat together until light and fluffy. In a separate bowl, combine the flour, baking soda, salt, cinnamon, ginger, cloves, and allspice. Slowly beat the flour mixture into the butter mixture.

Scoop the dough in teaspoon-size balls. Roll the cookies in the sugar, and lightly press them onto sheet pans lined with parchment paper. Bake for 8 to 10 minutes. Cool in the pans for a few minutes, then transfer to cooling racks and cool completely. Store in an airtight container.

Chocolate Gingersnaps

Chocolate is a wonderful addition to these classics.

Yield: 3 dozen cookies

3½ cups all-purpose flour
½ cup unsweetened cocoa powder
1 tablespoon baking soda
⅛ teaspoon salt
2 teaspoons ground cinnamon
2 teaspoons ground ginger
½ pound (2 sticks) butter, softened
1½ cups sugar
2 eggs
⅓ cup corn syrup

Preheat the oven to 350°F. In a large bowl, combine the flour, cocoa, baking soda, salt, cinnamon, and ginger. Using an electric mixer fitted with the paddle attachment, beat together the butter and sugar until light and fluffy. Add the eggs, one at a time, and then slowly add the corn syrup. Beat until light and fluffy. Slowly mix in the flour mixture.

Scoop teaspoonfuls of dough onto sheet pans lined with parchment paper. Lightly press them onto the pans with the back of a spoon. Bake for 8 to 10 minutes. Cool in the pans for a few minutes, then transfer to cooling racks and cool completely. Store in an airtight container.

Maple Birch Pecan Bars

The addition of birch syrup gives these bars a decidedly Alaskan flair.

Yield: 2 dozen bars

Crust
2¼ cups all-purpose flour
⅓ cup brown sugar
⅜ pound (1½ sticks) butter, softened

Filling
½ cup birch syrup
1½ cups maple syrup
½ cup brown sugar
4 eggs
¼ cup all-purpose flour
⅛ teaspoon salt
2 teaspoons vanilla extract
1½ cups chopped pecans

Preheat the oven to 350°F.

To make the crust: Butter a 9-by-13-inch baking pan. Using an electric mixer fitted with the paddle attachment, combine the flour, brown sugar, and butter. Mix together until the the consistency of fine crumbs. Gently press the mixture into the bottom of the prepared baking pan. Bake for 10 to 15 minutes, until the top of the crust is golden brown.

To make the filling: While the crust is baking, in a small saucepan over medium heat, simmer together the birch syrup, maple syrup, and brown sugar until the sugar is dissolved. Using an electric mixer fitted with the whisk attachment, whip the eggs until light. Slowly add the syrup mixture. Mix in the flour, salt, and vanilla. Pour over the prepared crust. Sprinkle the pecans over all.

Return the pan to the oven and bake for 20 to 25 minutes. Do not worry if the topping does not look totally set; it will continue to firm up once out of the oven. Allow to cool completely before cutting. Store in an airtight container.

Apricot Oatmeal Bars

Once, on a whim, we added white chocolate chips to these. They were such an instant hit that now we almost never make this recipe without them.

Yield: 32 bars

4 cups all-purpose flour
2 teaspoons baking soda
1½ teaspoons salt
3 cups rolled oats
2 teaspoons ground cinnamon
½ teaspoon ground allspice
1½ teaspoons ground nutmeg
1 teaspoon ground ginger
1 pound (4 sticks) butter, softened
1⅓ cups white sugar
1½ cups brown sugar
4 eggs
1 tablespoon vanilla extract
2 cups chopped dried apricots
1 tablespoon grated lemon zest
2 cups white chocolate chips (optional)
Orange Glaze (recipe follows)

Preheat the oven to 350°F. Butter a 9-by-13-inch baking pan. In a large bowl, combine the flour, baking soda, salt, oats, cinnamon, allspice, nutmeg, and ginger. Using an electric mixer fitted with the paddle attachment, beat together the butter, white sugar, and brown sugar until light and fluffy. Add the eggs one at a time, and then add the vanilla, mixing until light and fluffy. Slowly incorporate the flour mixture until thoroughly combined. Stir in the apricots, lemon zest, and white chocolate (if desired).

Spread the batter evenly in the prepared pan. Bake in the center of the oven for 30 to 40 minutes. Test the center for doneness with a toothpick. Cool completely before topping with Orange Glaze.

Orange Glaze

Yield: 1 cup

1 cup sugar
½ cup freshly squeezed orange juice
1 tablespoon grated orange zest

In a heavy-bottomed saucepan, mix together the sugar and orange juice. Cook over moderate heat until the sugar dissolves. Continue cooking until slightly thickened and the mixture has reduced to 1 cup. Remove from the heat and stir in the orange zest. Allow to cool slightly. Pour over the cooled Apricot Oatmeal Bars.

Oatmeal Tart Cherry Cookies

These are the cookies I always make for my father on Father's Day. A comforting classic is enhanced with the tart cherries.

Yield: 3 dozen cookies

2½ cups all-purpose flour
2 cups rolled oats
1 teaspoon baking soda
⅛ teaspoon salt
2 teaspoons ground cinnamon
½ teaspoon ground allspice
1 teaspoon ground nutmeg
1 teaspoon ground ginger
½ pound (2 sticks) butter, softened
¾ cup brown sugar
¾ cup white sugar
2 eggs
1 tablespoon vanilla extract
1½ cups dried tart or sour cherries

Optional
1½ cups chopped dark chocolate

Preheat the oven to 350°F. In a large bowl, combine the flour, oats, baking soda, salt, cinnamon, allspice, nutmeg, and ginger. Using an electric mixer fitted with the paddle attachment, beat together the butter, brown sugar, and white sugar until light and fluffy. Add the eggs, one at a time, and then add the vanilla. Beat until light and fluffy. Slowly incorporate the flour mixture until thoroughly combined. Stir in the cherries, and chocolate (optional).

Scoop teaspoonfuls of dough onto sheet pans lined with parchment paper. Bake for 10 to 12 minutes. Cool in the pans or a cooling rack. Store in an airtight container.

Orange Chocolate Chunk Cookies

These Viennese inspired cookies are a great mid-morning treat with a cup of hot tea.

Yield: 2½ dozen cookies

2 cups all-purpose flour
1 cup rolled oats
⅛ teaspoon salt
1 teaspoon baking soda
2 teaspoons ground cinnamon
⅜ pound (1½ sticks) butter, softened
¾ cup white sugar
¾ cup brown sugar
2 eggs
2 teaspoons vanilla extract
1½ tablespoons freshly squeezed orange juice
1 tablespoon grated orange zest
8 ounces semisweet chocolate, broken into pieces

Preheat the oven to 350°F. In a large bowl, combine the flour, oats, salt, baking soda, and cinnamon. Using an electric mixer fitted with the paddle attachment, beat together the butter, white sugar, and brown sugar until light and fluffy. Add the eggs one at a time, beating until light and fluffy. Slowly mix in the vanilla and orange juice, and then slowly add the flour/oat mixture. Mix until thoroughly combined. Mix in the orange zest and dark chocolate.

Scoop teaspoonfuls of dough onto sheet pans lined with parchment paper. Bake for 10 to 12 minutes. Cool in the pans or on a cooling rack. Store in an airtight container.

The Evening Meal

This is the land of midnight sun, where summer dining hours are never rushed with the threat of approaching darkness. It is a time to share stories of adventures had that day. Of course, the camaraderie is enhanced by the wonderful food. When weather permits, we gather outside in the evening to relax in the shadow of Mount McKinley. Our guests have spent the day exploring the splendor of the park, and in doing so they have caught a glimpse of the delicate infrastructure and web of life that make this park unique. After a quick shower, with appetite in tow, they settle into a leisurely evening of fantastic food and great company.

Hors d'Oeuvres

We love creating eclectic little tasters to tempt the appetite. These are daily creations, made with the freshest ingredients and greenhouse goodies. The following recipes range from simple, quick, casual fare, to more time-consuming elegant hors d'oeuvres.

Smoked Salmon Spirals

The thinner the slices of smoked salmon, the more dramatic these spirals will look. For a more formal affair, garnish them with dill and salmon roe.

Yield: 30 hors d'oeuvres

¾ cup (5 ounces) cream cheese
¼ cup chopped chives or scallion greens
2 tablespoons chopped fresh dill
1 tablespoon sour cream
1 teaspoon Dijon mustard
1 teaspoon grated lemon zest
½ pound thinly sliced smoked salmon
30 thin, crispy crackers

In a bowl, mix together the cream cheese, chives or scallions, dill, sour cream, mustard, and lemon zest. Lay a piece of plastic wrap, about 18 inches long, on a clean work surface. Place the salmon lengthwise on the plastic wrap, and spread the cream cheese mixture evenly over the salmon, leaving ¼ inch uncovered at the top. Using the plastic wrap as an aid, roll the salmon up tightly to form a spiral. Wrap tightly with plastic wrap. Freeze for 20 minutes to set the spiral. Remove the plastic wrap and, using a very sharp knife, cut the spiral crosswise into ⅓-inch-thick slices. Set the spirals on crackers and serve.

Onion Cheese Puffs

These are best when served immediately.

Yield: 32 hors d'oeuvres

¾ cup minced yellow onion
½ cup mayonnaise
2 tablespoons grated Swiss cheese
3 tablespoons grated Parmesan cheese
2 tablespoons chopped fresh parsley
⅛ teaspoon kosher salt
Freshly ground black pepper
8 slices white bread

Preheat the oven to 350°F. In a bowl, mix together the onion, mayonnaise, Swiss and Parmesan cheeses, and parsley. Season with the salt and pepper to taste.

Remove the crusts from the bread. Using a 1-inch round cookie cutter, cut the bread into 32 rounds. Place on a sheet pan and bake, without turning, until golden, 10 to 15 minutes. Preheat the broiler. Onto each bread round, spread 1 teaspoon of the onion/cheese mixture. Brown under the broiler for 1 to 2 minutes. Serve immediately.

Vegetable Sushi

Simple elegance describes this hors d'oeuvre. You will need an inexpensive bamboo roller to form the rolls.

Yield: 48 hors d'oeuvres

2¾ cups uncooked sushi rice (yields about 6 cups cooked rice)
3 cups water
¼ cup mirin
1 medium carrot, peeled
1 red bell pepper
1 English cucumber, peeled
2 scallions
6 sheets nori (dried seaweed)
2 teaspoons wasabi paste
8 ounces sliced pickled ginger
Sushi Dipping Sauce (recipe follows)

Rinse the rice under cold running water. Drain well. Place the rice and water in a medium saucepan and set over high heat. Cover, bring to a boil, and reduce the heat. Cook until the rice is tender, about 15 minutes. Turn off the heat and remove the lid. Sprinkle the rice with some of the mirin. Replace the lid and let the rice sit for 15 minutes. Transfer to a bowl, and allow to cool to room temperature.

Cut the carrot, bell pepper, cucumber, and scallions into ¼-by-3-inch matchsticks. Lay a sheet of nori on a bamboo mat. Sprinkle with some of the mirin. Spread 1 cup cooked rice on the nori, leaving a ½-inch border at each end. Spread ⅓ teaspoon wasabi paste in a horizontal strip across the middle of the rice. Place an assortment of the matchstick-cut vegetables on top of the wasabi paste. Cover with a layer of ginger. Using the closest end of the bamboo roller, roll up the sushi to form a spiral, pressing firmly on the mat as you roll. Remove and cover loosely with a moist paper towel and repeat with the remaining ingredients. Using a very sharp knife, trim the ends of the rolls. Cut each roll into 8 equal pieces. Serve with the dipping sauce.

Sushi Dipping Sauce

This is also a tasty sauce to serve with grilled chicken satays.

Yield: ¾ cup

1 teaspoon wasabi paste
2 teaspoons scallion greens, thinly sliced diagonally
½ cup mirin
6 tablespoons soy sauce
1 teaspoon dark sesame oil

In a small bowl, combine the wasabi, scallions, mirin, and soy sauce. Slowly mix in the sesame oil. Stir until well combined. Serve with Vegetable Sushi.

Spicy Almond Dip

Serve with the crackers or toasted bread of your choice.

Yield: 3 cups

2 cups dry-roasted salted almonds
2 tablespoons almond oil
2 teaspoons dry mustard
2 teaspoons Worcestershire sauce
1 teaspoon cayenne pepper
½ cup sour cream
½ cup mayonnaise
½ cup chopped scallion greens

In a food processor, purée together the almonds and almond oil until a thick paste is formed. Using a rubber spatula, scoop the almond butter into a medium-size bowl. Add the dry mustard, Worcestershire sauce, cayenne, sour cream, mayonnaise, and scallion greens, mixing until thoroughly combined. Store in the refrigerator until ready to use. Garnish with additional chopped scallion greens.

Cheese Straws

Serve these with thick Cilantro Gazpacho. The recipe follows. Try making Cheese Straws with blue cheese and serving them as an accompaniment to spinach salad.

Yield: 24 straws

4 ounces sharp cheddar cheese, grated
¼ teaspoon cayenne
2 tablespoons chopped fresh parsley
1 sheet puff pastry
1 egg
2 teaspoons water
⅛ teaspoon sea salt

Preheat the oven to 425°F. In a small bowl, toss together the cheddar cheese, cayenne, and parsley. On a lightly floured surface, roll out the puff pastry into a 14-by-12-inch rectangle. Cut it in half crosswise, forming two 7-by-12-inch rectangles.

In a small bowl, mix together the egg and water. Brush the pastry with some of this egg wash. Sprinkle the cheese mixture over 1 sheet of the pastry. Top with the second sheet of pastry, pressing down on it gently to remove any air. Brush the top with egg wash and sprinkle with the sea salt.

With a sharp knife or pastry wheel, cut the pastry into strips ½-inch wide. Twist the strips and arrange them on sheet pans lined with parchment paper. Press down on the ends so they will retain their shape when baked.

Bake for 10 to 12 minutes. Allow to cool in the pan for a few minutes. Serve, or store in an airtight container.

Cilantro Gazpacho

Cilantro enhances the crisp, fresh flavor of gazpacho.

Yield: 3 cups (enough to serve 12 people as an hors d'oeuvre with Cheese Straws)

½ cup minced red onion
½ cup chopped fresh cilantro
1 cup diced Roma tomatoes
½ cup peeled, diced cucumber
½ cup diced zucchini
1 tablespoon kosher salt
1 tablespoon minced fresh jalapeño chile
1 tablespoon fresh lime juice
1 teaspoon crushed garlic

In a small bowl, soak the onion in water to cover for 20 minutes. Drain and rinse well. In a larger bowl, stir together all of the ingredients, including the onion. Let the gazpacho sit at room temperature for 30 minutes to allow the flavors to combine. Serve in bowls, accompanied by Cheese Straws.

Raita with Crispy Radishes

Radish roses are the crisp, colorful accompaniment to this cucumber yogurt dip.
For a heartier appetizer, serve the raita with pita triangles.

Yield: 1½ cups

¾ cup plain yogurt
½ cup peeled, diced cucumber
¼ cup sour cream
¼ cup chiffonade (thin strips) of fresh mint leaves
3 tablespoons minced red onion
1½ teaspoons rice wine vinegar
1 teaspoon fresh lime juice
½ teaspoon grated fresh ginger
½ teaspoon grated lime zest
1 teaspoon kosher salt
1 teaspoon ground cumin
1 tablespoon freshly ground pepper
24 radishes

In a medium-size bowl, combine all ingredients, except the radishes. Mix well to thoroughly combine. Set in the refrigerator for at least 1 hour to allow the flavors to combine.

Cut a deep X into the root end of each radish, and transfer to a bowl of ice water. Refrigerate the radishes until they open up, about 1 hour. Drain and rinse the radishes. Serve with Raita.

Parmesan Crisps with Radicchio and Ripe Pears

This is a wonderful and easy appetizer for fall, when pears are at their very best. You can make the cheese crisps in advance and store them at room temperature in an airtight container.

Yield: 24 hors d'oeuvres

3 cups grated Parmesan cheese
6 firm, ripe pears
2 heads radicchio, cleaned, leaves torn loose
1 teaspoon freshly ground pepper

Preheat the oven to 375°F. On a sheet pan lined with parchment paper, lightly draw six circles, about 2½ inches in diameter, on the parchment paper with a nontoxic pen. Sprinkle 2 tablespoons of Parmesan cheese into and covering each circle. Bake for 7 to 10 minutes, until the cheese is golden and bubbly. The edges should be slightly darker than the interior. Remove from the oven and allow to cool in the pan. When the cheese is firm, remove it from pan. Repeat with the remaining cheese.

Cut each pear into 12 pieces. Top each cheese crisp with some radicchio and slices of pear. Sprinkle with pepper.

Bruschetta

Try this Italian-style fried bread as a vehicle for a variety of toppings.

Yield: About 36 toasts

¼ to ½ cup olive oil
1 loaf crusty French or Italian bread (about 24 inches long)
1 large clove garlic
Tapenade Topping for Bruschetta or Tomato-Parmesan Topping
   for Bruschetta (recipes follow)

    Heat ¼ cup of oil in a large sauté pan. Using a serrated knife, cut the bread crosswise on a slight diagonal into ½-inch-thick slices. Line a sheet pan with paper towels, and place it near the sauté pan. When the oil is hot enough (almost smoking), gently set slices of bread in the pan. Working in batches of 8 to 10 slices at a time, fry the bread for about 1 minute, until the pan side of the bread is slightly golden. (This happens very fast, so watch carefully.) Transfer the bread to the paper towels. Continue frying the remaining bread, replenishing oil as needed. Rub the fried toasts with garlic and spread with the topping of your choice.

Tapenade Topping for Bruschetta

Olives are the key ingredient in this topping. Good-quality olives will have firm flesh and will not be too salty. If you are unsure what to buy, just ask your grocer if you can taste some olives. You are always the best judge of your own palate.

Yield: 2½ cups

¼ cup olive oil
1 large clove garlic
1 cup pitted green olives (French picholine olives preferred)
1 cup pitted kalamata olives
1 tablespoon grated lemon zest
1 tablespoon fresh lemon juice
¼ cup sun-dried tomatoes
¼ cup fresh basil leaves

In the bowl of a food processor, combine all ingredients. Pulse the machine to combine. The mixture should retain a slightly chunky texture. Spoon onto Bruschetta and serve.

Tomato-Parmesan Topping for Bruschetta

This is also a wonderful topping for flatbread or pizza.

Yield: 2½ cups

2 tablespoons olive oil
⅓ cup minced shallots
1½ cups diced Roma tomatoes
2 tablespoons grated lemon zest
½ cup chopped fresh parsley
½ cup grated Parmesan cheese
1 teaspoon kosher salt
1 teaspoon freshly ground black pepper

Heat the oil in a large skillet over medium-high heat. Add the shallots and sauté until light golden in color. Reduce the heat and add the tomatoes. Continue cooking until liquid forms but tomatoes are still chunky. Add the lemon zest and parsley.

Remove from the heat and cool to room temperature. When cool, strain off the excess juice. Add the Parmesan cheese, salt, and pepper. Spoon the topping onto Bruschetta and serve.

Herbed Cream Cheese with Salmon Roe

Herbed cream cheese can also be used as a condiment for a roast beef sandwich.

Yield: 2 cups

1 cup (8 ounces) cream cheese, softened
½ cup sour cream
1 tablespoon Dijon mustard
2 teaspoons garlic salt
1 tablespoon chopped fresh thyme
1 tablespoon chopped fresh tarragon
1 tablespoon chiffonade (thin strips) of fresh basil
1 tablespoon chopped fresh dill
1 tablespoon chopped fresh oregano
1 tablespoon chopped fresh parsley
½ teaspoon cayenne
2 ounces salmon roe

Using an electric mixer fitted with the paddle attachment, beat the cream cheese until very smooth. Add the sour cream, mustard, garlic salt, thyme, tarragon, basil, dill, oregano, parsley, and cayenne. Mix until thoroughly combined. Spoon onto Bruschetta and top with the salmon roe.

Phyllo Dough

Literally translated, the Greek word "phyllo" means "leaf." In culinary terms, it refers to paper-thin dough similar to strudel dough. Found fresh in Greek specialty markets, it is also available frozen in most supermarkets. Phyllo can be tricky to work with, so here are a few hints: Store phyllo unopened in the refrigerator for up to one month and in the freezer for up to one year. Once you open a package of phyllo, it is best to use it all at once. Refreezing will make it brittle. When working with phyllo, cover the unused sheets loosely with a damp towel to keep them from drying out.

Crab and Brie Phyllo Cigars

If you don't need this many hors d'oeuvres, freeze the extras unbaked. When you're ready to use them, no thawing is required. They can go right from the freezer to the oven.

Yield: 50 hors d'oeuvres

1 pound Brie
1 cup (8 ounces) cream cheese
2 cups lump crabmeat, drained and picked over for shells
1 teaspoon kosher salt
½ teaspoon cayenne
½ teaspoon paprika
½ cup chopped fresh parsley plus some for garnish
½ cup chopped scallion greens
½ pound (2 sticks) butter
1 (16-ounce) package phyllo dough, thawed

Preheat the oven to 400°F. Cube the Brie and cream cheese. In a large bowl, combine the cubed cheeses, crab, salt, cayenne, paprika, parsley, and scallions. Mix to thoroughly combine, and set aside.

In a small saucepan, melt the butter. Stack 3 sheets of phyllo dough, brushing each sheet with butter to coat it evenly. Cut the stack lengthwise into 5 strips. Set a dollop of filling at the base of each strip. Roll up the strips while gently applying pressure to form cigar shapes about 2 to 3 inches in length. Place the cigars onto a sheet pan lined with parchment paper. Repeat with the remaining phyllo and filling.

Bake for 10 to 15 minutes, until the phyllo is a light golden color. Allow to cool in the pans for 5 minutes. Garnish with chopped parsley and serve.

Spanakopita

This savory pie makes a great vegetarian entrée. Like the Crab and Brie Phyllo Cigars, these can be frozen, unbaked, and baked without thawing.

Yield: 48 hors d'oeuvres

½ cup minced yellow onion
1 teaspoon minced garlic
1 tablespoon olive oil
12 cups baby spinach
1 tablespoon chopped fresh oregano
1 cup crumbled feta cheese
2 eggs, beaten
1 teaspoon kosher salt
1 teaspoon freshly ground pepper
½ pound (2 sticks) butter
1 (16-ounce) package phyllo, thawed

In a large skillet over medium-high heat, sauté the onion and garlic in the olive oil. When the onion and garlic are slightly golden, add the spinach and oregano. Working fast, add spinach in batches to coat with the hot oil and onions. Remove from the heat, allowing the residual heat in the pan to continue wilting the spinach. When cool, add the feta and eggs, and season with salt and pepper. Strain off the excess liquid and set aside.

Preheat the oven to 400°F. In a small saucepan, melt the butter. Stack 4 sheets of phyllo, brushing each sheet to coat it evenly with butter. Cut the stack lengthwise into 6 strips. Set a dollop of filling at the base of each strip. Turn and fold the phyllo over the filling, completely enclosing the filling and forming a triangle shape as you do so. Set the triangles on a sheet pan lined with parchment paper. Repeat with the remaining phyllo and filling.

Brush the tops with melted butter. Bake for 10 to 15 minutes, until the phyllo is a light golden color. Allow to cool in the pan for 5 minutes. Serve hot or at room temperature.

Grilled Chicken Satay

Flank steak also works well in this Indonesian-inspired dish.

Yield: 30 skewers

¼ cup fresh lime juice
¼ cup vegetable oil
¼ cup soy sauce
2 tablespoons dark sesame oil
2 tablespoons minced ginger
1 tablespoon minced garlic
¼ cup brown sugar
1 tablespoon crushed red pepper flakes
2 pounds boneless, skinless chicken breasts
Satay Dipping Sauce (recipe follows)

In a large bowl, combine the lime juice, oil, soy sauce, sesame oil, ginger, garlic, brown sugar, and red pepper flakes. Whisk together. Add the chicken, turn to coat, and cover bowl with plastic wrap. Refrigerate for at least 6 hours or overnight.

Preheat a grill or ridged grill pan. Arrange the chicken on the grill or in the pan. Grill for about 10 minutes on each side. Transfer to a cutting board and allow to cool. When cool, slice the chicken on a slight diagonal, ½ inch thick, halving the longer slices. Thread onto bamboo skewers. Serve with Satay Dipping Sauce.

Satay Dipping Sauce

You can make this in advance and store it in the refrigerator for up to 1 week. Bring to room temperature and whisk well to combine ingredients.

Yield: 1½ cups

2 teaspoons dark sesame oil
1 teaspoon olive oil
¼ cup minced yellow onion
2 teaspoons minced garlic
1½ teaspoons minced fresh ginger
¼ teaspoon crushed red pepper flakes
½ cup smooth peanut butter
¼ cup dark brown sugar
2 tablespoons white wine vinegar
2 tablespoons soy sauce
1 tablespoon ketchup
1½ teaspoons fresh lime juice

In a small saucepan over medium heat, combine the sesame oil and olive oil. Add the onion, garlic, ginger, and pepper flakes. Sauté until very aromatic, about 8 minutes. In a small bowl, combine the peanut butter, brown sugar, vinegar, soy sauce, ketchup, and lime juice. Whisk the peanut butter mixture into the onion mixture. Continue to cook for 1 minute. Transfer to a bowl and let cool. Serve with Grilled Chicken Satay.

Herbed Cucumber Dip with Borage Blossoms

Both flowers and leaves of the borage plant are edible. The bright, blue-purple color and sweet cucumber flavor of borage blossoms garnish this dip, which you can use as part of a vegetable crudité platter or with toasted pita bread.

We grow a variety of edible flowers in our greenhouse. Incorporate them yourself in cooking or as garnishes to transform even the most everyday dish into something special. Some farmers' markets and even supermarkets now carry edible flowers. You can also find specialty cookbooks and gardening books to guide you.

Yield: 3 cups

1 large cucumber, peeled, seeded, and diced
1 teaspoon rice wine vinegar
1 teaspoon soy sauce
3 dashes bitters
½ teaspoon sugar
½ teaspoon salt
½ teaspoon white pepper
1 teaspoon minced garlic
2 tablespoons chopped fresh parsley
1 tablespoon chiffonade (thin strips) of fresh basil
2 tablespoons chopped fresh dill
1⅓ cups sour cream
¾ cup yogurt
20 borage blossoms

In a large bowl, mix together the cucumber, vinegar, soy sauce, bitters, sugar, salt, and pepper. Mix well and let stand for 5 minutes. Add the garlic, parsley, basil, and dill, and mix well. Add the sour cream and yogurt, and mix well. Refrigerate for 30 minutes to allow the flavors to combine. Garnish with the borage blossoms and serve.

Shrimp with Chipotle Aioli

This is a great alternative to the classic shrimp cocktail. Shrimp are marketed and sold according to size/number per pound. This recipe calls for 2 pounds of large shrimp, estimating 21 to 25 per pound, served as an hors d'oeuvre. That should be a good amount for 15 people. If you have some real shrimp lovers in the crowd, you might want to increase the amount of shrimp.

Serves 15 as an hors d'oeuvre

2 pounds large cooked shrimp, peeled and deveined, tails left on
2 canned chipotle chiles in adobo sauce
1 teaspoon adobo sauce
1 cup mayonnaise
1 cup sour cream
1 tablespoon Dijon mustard
3 tablespoons chopped fresh cilantro
Cilantro sprigs

Rinse the shrimp well under cold running water. Drain and pat dry with paper towels. Set aside. Using a food processor, purée the chiles with the adobo sauce to form a paste. Set aside. In a separate bowl, mix together the mayonnaise, sour cream, mustard, and cilantro. Mix in the reserved chipotle paste. Transfer to a serving bowl, set the bowl on a platter and surround it with the shrimp. Garnish with cilantro sprigs and serve.

Soups

It has often been said that soup is food for the soul. We couldn't agree more. Whether it is hot or cold, thick or thin, smooth or chunky, sweet or savory, soup is always comforting. To make a great soup is a labor of love. Rarely does it rely on precise measurements and exact quantities. It is important to use the best possible ingredients to enhance the delicate balance of flavors that defines a great soup. Most importantly, always taste your soup as you make it, adjusting any seasonings according to your preference.

A good stock is the base of most soups. It is wonderful, but not always practical, to make your own. Fortunately, many good-quality stocks, broths, and bouillons are available in the markets. If using bouillon cubes or canned broths, search out superior quality. Many of them tend to be very salty. Make your soup in a good-quality stockpot; never use aluminum, as it can discolor some vegetables and impart a "tin can" flavor. Although no special tools are needed to make great soup, a handheld blender is useful for making a puréed soup or bisque because it can be immersed directly into the pot of soup.

The following are just a few of our favorite recipes. Make them as they are or use them as an outline to aid in your own creation. We are sure you will enjoy them either way.

Saffron Soup

Saffron is the stamen of a small purple crocus, and there are about 14,000 threads per ounce. Although saffron is very expensive, you need just a few threads to transform any dish. Always buy saffron in the thread form rather than the powder, which has often been adulterated. Store saffron in a cool, dark place and it will keep for up to a year. The saffron in this very simple soup adds a subtle, delicate flavor and a beautiful golden color.

Yield: 12 cups, 8 servings

2 tablespoons butter
1 yellow onion, minced
3½ cups potatoes, peeled and diced
2 cups rich chicken stock
4 cups whole milk
½ teaspoon saffron threads
2 cups heavy cream
1 teaspoon kosher salt
½ teaspoon cayenne
1 tablespoon chopped fresh parsley
1 tablespoon chopped fresh chives
1 tablespoon chopped fresh tarragon

In a heavy-bottomed stockpot, melt the butter over medium-high heat. Add the onion and sauté until tender. Add the potatoes and chicken stock. Bring to a boil, reduce the heat, and simmer for 10 minutes. Add the milk and simmer for 15 minutes. When the potatoes are tender, purée the soup. Run the mixture through a sieve to ensure a smooth texture. Return it to a simmer and stir in the saffron and cream. Season with the salt and cayenne. Taste and adjust the seasonings. Continue to simmer for 10 minutes. Serve the soup garnished with the fresh parsley, chives, and tarragon.

Parsnip Bisque with Hazelnut Pesto

Parsnips are perfectly suited to Alaskan cooking. This creamy white root retains a delicate, sweet, gingery flavor, even though it has an extremely long shelf life. This soup is intended to be served hot but can also be served cold if you substitute milk for the heavy cream.

Yield: 12 cups, 8 servings

6 leeks, white and pale green parts only
4 tablespoons butter
2 cups minced shallots
1 cup diced celery
2 pounds parsnips, peeled and diced
½ cup dry sherry, divided
8 cups vegetable stock
½ cup heavy cream
1 tablespoon kosher salt
2 teaspoons white pepper
¾ cup hazelnuts, toasted and chopped
Hazelnut Pesto (recipe follows)

Cut the leeks in half lengthwise, and rinse well to remove all dirt. Mince and set aside. In a large, heavy-bottomed stockpot, melt the butter over medium-high heat. Add the shallots, leeks, and celery. Sauté until slightly golden and tender. Add the parsnips and stir to coat with butter. Sauté until slightly browned. Deglaze the pot with ¼ cup of the sherry. Add the vegetable stock and reduce the heat to low. Cover the pot and simmer for 20 minutes, until all of the vegetables are very soft. Purée the mixture. Stir in the remaining ¼ cup sherry and the cream. Season with the salt and pepper. Taste and adjust the seasonings. Serve the soup in bowls, garnished with the toasted hazelnuts and topped with a dollop of Hazelnut Pesto.

Hazelnut Pesto

Store this pesto in the refrigerator or freeze it for later use.

Yield: 2 cups

1 tablespoon minced garlic
2 teaspoons kosher salt
1 cup hazelnuts, toasted and chopped
2 cups chopped fresh parsley
¾ cup olive oil
2 tablespoons hazelnut oil
1 teaspoon freshly ground pepper

Using a food processor, purée together the garlic and salt to form a paste.
Add the hazelnuts and parsley. Purée again to form a paste. Slowly incorporate
the olive and hazelnut oils. Purée until well blended and smooth. Add the pepper.
Serve with Parsnip Bisque.

Black Bean Pumpkin Soup

Although black beans and pumpkin might sound like an odd combination, the flavors complement each other beautifully. This soup becomes an autumn delight when served in hollowed-out roasted petite pumpkins.

Yield: 12 cups, 8 servings

4 tablespoons butter
1½ cups minced red onion
¼ cup minced garlic
2 tablespoons ground cumin
1 tablespoon dark chili powder
2 teaspoons kosher salt
2 teaspoons crushed red pepper flakes
4½ cups cooked black beans,
    rinsed and drained
½ cup flat beer, amber or porter
3 cups diced tomatoes
1 (16-ounce) can pumpkin purée
4 cups rich chicken stock
½ cup chopped scallion greens
1 cup chopped fresh cilantro
1 cup sour cream
12 ounces bacon, cooked until crisp and broken into bits
1 cup toasted, shelled pumpkin seeds

In a large, heavy-bottomed stockpot, melt the butter over medium-high heat. Add the onion and garlic, and sauté until tender and light golden. Stir in the cumin, chili powder, salt, and red pepper flakes, and sauté until very aromatic. Stir in the black beans, and turn to coat them completely with the onion mixture. Deglaze the stockpot with the beer. Stir in the tomatoes and then the pumpkin purée. Continue stirring to combine well. Slowly start to incorporate the chicken stock, stirring to combine completely. Reduce the heat and simmer for 15 minutes, stirring often. Add the scallions and cilantro. Serve the soup in bowls, garnished with the sour cream, bacon, and pumpkin seeds.

Carrot Ginger Bisque

By definition, bisques are soups or purées thickened with cream. In this recipe, the purée of carrots is the thickener, making it a much healthier alternative.

Yield: 12 cups, 8 to 10 servings

3 tablespoons butter
3 tablespoons olive oil
1 yellow onion, diced
1½ pounds carrots, peeled and diced (4½ cups)
1½ cups dry white wine
1 tablespoon minced fresh ginger
1 tablespoon minced garlic
6 cups rich chicken stock
2 teaspoons kosher salt
1 teaspoon freshly ground pepper
1 tablespoon ground ginger
1 cup Crème Fraîche (recipe follows)
½ cup chopped fresh chives

In a large, heavy-bottomed stockpot, melt the butter and oil over medium-high heat. Add the onion and sauté until soft. Add the carrots and continue to sauté for 10 minutes. Deglaze the pot with a little of the wine. Add the minced ginger and garlic. Sauté for 2 minutes, stirring constantly. Add the remaining wine and increase the heat. Simmer until the wine has reduced by half. Add the chicken stock and reduce the heat to low. Simmer for 25 minutes until the carrots are very soft. Purée the soup until very smooth. Add the salt, pepper, and ground ginger. Taste and adjust the seasonings. Top each bowl with a hearty dollop of Crème Fraîche, and sprinkle with chives.

Crème Fraîche

Crème fraîche adds richness and depth to Carrot Ginger Bisque. You can buy it in some gourmet markets, but it is very expensive, and you can easily make a superior version at home. Crème fraîche will keep in the refrigerator for up to 2 weeks.

Yield: 1 cup

1 cup heavy cream
2 tablespoons buttermilk

Mix together the heavy cream and buttermilk. Place in a glass container and cover. Let stand at room temperature for 8 to 24 hours, until very thick. Stir well and refrigerate.

Five-Onion Soup

This is our adaptation of the classic French onion soup. Caramelizing the onions gives this soup a rich onion base.

Yield: 8 cups, 8 servings

1 loaf crusty French Baguette
2 leeks, white and pale green parts only
3 tablespoons butter
1 tablespoon olive oil
1 yellow onion, thinly sliced
1 red onion, thinly sliced
5 shallots, thinly sliced
1 teaspoon kosher salt
1 tablespoon sugar
3 tablespoons all-purpose flour
¼ cup Madeira
8 cups rich beef stock
1 teaspoon freshly ground pepper
2 cups grated Gruyère cheese
1 cup chopped scallion greens

Using a serrated knife, cut the bread crosswise on a slight diagonal, into ½-inch-thick slices. You should have 16 slices. Toast the bread and set aside.

Cut the leeks in half lengthwise, rinse well to remove all dirt, mince, and set aside. In a large, heavy-bottomed stockpot, melt the butter with the olive oil over medium-high heat. Add the leeks, yellow and red onions, and shallots. Sauté until tender and slightly golden. Sprinkle the salt and sugar over the onion mixture. Stir to coat the onions. Stop stirring and sauté the onions for 3 minutes. Gently turn the onions in the pan to caramelize them. Reduce the heat to low and sprinkle with the flour. Turn to coat and let the mixture cook for 3 minutes.

Deglaze the pot with some of the Madeira. Slowly start stirring in the beef stock. Continue stirring until all the stock is added. Add the remaining Madeira and the pepper. Allow to simmer for 45 minutes. Taste and adjust the seasonings.

Place 1 slice of toasted bread in the bottom of each bowl, and sprinkle each slice with 1 tablespoon of the grated cheese. Spoon the soup and onions on top of the bread. The bread should rise to the top of the soup. Top this with another piece of bread, sprinkle the remaining cheese on top, and place the bowls under a broiler for 2 minutes. The cheese should be bubbly and golden. Serve garnished with scallion greens.

Curried Squash and Pear Bisque

Curry powder is a pulverized blend of up to 20 different spices, herbs, and seeds. Among those most commonly used are cardamom, chiles, cinnamon, cloves, coriander, cumin, fennel seeds, fenugreek, mace, nutmeg, red and black pepper, poppy and sesame seeds, saffron, tamarind, and turmeric. It is the saffron and turmeric that give curry its golden yellow color. Curry powder quickly loses its pungency. When stored in an airtight container, it is good for only 2 months.

Yield: 12 cups, 8 servings

1 large butternut squash, about 3 pounds
3 tablespoons butter, divided
1½ cups thinly sliced Spanish onion
1 pound Bartlett pears, peeled and diced, plus 1 Bartlett pear,
  cored and thinly sliced
1 tablespoon curry powder
1 cup pear nectar
6 cups rich chicken stock
1 cup coconut milk
½ cup heavy cream
1 teaspoon kosher salt
1 teaspoon freshly ground pepper
½ teaspoon paprika
½ teaspoon ground cinnamon

Preheat the oven to 375°F. Cut the squash in half lengthwise, and remove and discard the seeds and membrane. Generously butter a casserole dish, using 1 tablespoon of the butter. Place the squash, cut sides down, in the dish. Cover with foil and bake for 25 minutes or until the pulp is very soft. Remove from the oven and remove the foil. Allow to cool and scoop out the pulp; set aside.

In a large, heavy-bottomed stockpot, melt the rest of the butter over medium-high heat. Add the onion and sauté until lightly browned. Add the diced pears and curry powder, and stir to combine. Sauté until very aromatic. Add the reserved squash pulp and pear nectar. Reduce the heat, stirring to combine all ingredients. Slowly incorporate the chicken stock, stirring constantly. Purée the soup, and then add the coconut milk and cream. Return to a simmer. Add the salt and pepper. Taste and adjust the seasonings. Serve in bowls, garnished with pear slices and sprinkled with paprika and cinnamon.

Minted Pea Soup

This light, fresh-tasting soup is also delicious chilled.

Yield: 10 cups, 6 to 8 servings

Croutons
4 slices whole-grain sandwich bread
1 tablespoon olive oil

Soup
3 tablespoons butter
1 tablespoon olive oil
1 cup minced shallots
1 pound Yukon Gold potatoes, peeled and diced
4 cups rich chicken stock
2 (10-ounce) packages frozen peas
1 cup fresh mint leaves
2 cups julienned snow peas
2 teaspoons kosher salt
2 teaspoons freshly ground pepper
½ cup pea shoots (available in specialty markets)

To make the croutons: Preheat the oven to 400°F. Cut the bread into 1-inch cubes, and toss with the olive oil. Spread the bread evenly on a sheet pan. Bake until golden brown, 10 minutes. Remove from the oven and set aside.

To make the soup: In a large, heavy-bottomed stockpot, melt the butter and olive oil over medium-high heat. Add the shallots and sauté until tender. Add the potatoes, and turn to coat them with butter. Add the chicken stock, and bring to a boil. Reduce the heat and simmer for 20 minutes, until the potatoes are very tender. Add the frozen peas and mint. Simmer for 3 minutes. The peas should be tender and still bright green. Purée the soup until smooth. Add the snow peas and return to a simmer. Season with the salt and pepper, taste, and adjust the seasonings. Serve in bowls, garnished with the croutons and fresh pea shoots.

Artichoke and Parmesan Soup with White Truffle Oil

Truffles, both white and black, have been prized by gourmets for centuries. Growing wild in northern Italy and France, these fungi are rare and difficult to find, and their harvesting season is limited. Because truffles are very expensive, we recommend using truffle oil. The earthy, garlicky, pungent flavor of fresh truffles is wonderfully preserved in this oil, which you can find at most specialty markets. It is still expensive, but a little goes a long way.

Yield: 10 cups, 6 servings

36 ounces canned artichoke hearts, drained
¼ cup olive oil
1 cup minced shallots
1½ cups dry white wine
6 cups rich chicken stock
1 teaspoon kosher salt
1 teaspoon freshly ground pepper
4-ounce chunk Parmesan cheese
3 tablespoons butter
¼ cup white truffle oil

Rinse the artichoke hearts well and drain.

In a large, heavy-bottomed stockpot, heat the olive oil over medium-high heat. Add the shallots and sauté for 2 minutes, until slightly golden and tender. Add the artichoke hearts, and turn to coat them with the oil. Sauté over medium heat for 2 minutes. Add the wine and simmer for 10 minutes. Once the wine has reduced by half, add the chicken stock, reduce the heat, cover, and simmer for 20 minutes. Season with the salt and pepper. Purée the soup. Taste and adjust the seasonings. If the soup is too thick, add more chicken stock. Slice the cheese, using a vegetable peeler. Whisk in the butter just before serving. Serve the soup in bowls, with truffle oil drizzled over it in a circular motion and slices of Parmesan cheese on top.

Spicy Tomato Soup

Food historian M. F. K. Fisher was quoted as saying of tomatoes, "The best way to eat them is in the garden, warm and pungent from the vine." Unfortunately, many of us in northern climates do not have that luxury. Instead of buying the bland, perfectly shaped but flavorless tomatoes that grocery stores carry, we recommend finding a good-quality canned tomato. The flavor is more truly tomato. Cilantro adds a refreshing taste to this spicy soup. Serve either hot or cold.

Yield: 10 cups, 6 servings

2 tablespoons olive oil
1 red onion, diced
1 tablespoon minced garlic
1½ teaspoons kosher salt
2 teaspoons crushed red pepper flakes
½ jalapeño chile, seeded and minced (use caution when handling)
2 (28-ounce) cans crushed plum tomatoes in juice
1 teaspoon sugar
2 tablespoons fresh lime juice
2 cups rich chicken stock
1 cup chopped fresh cilantro, stems included
½ cup chiffonade (thin strips) of fresh basil
¼ cup sour cream

In a large, heavy-bottomed stockpot, heat the oil over medium-high heat. Add the onion and garlic, and sauté until tender and slightly golden. Add the salt and red pepper flakes, stirring to combine. Add the jalapeño and sauté until tender. Add the tomatoes and their juice. Simmer over high heat for 10 minutes. When the liquid is reduced by one-fourth, stir in the sugar and lime juice, and then stir in the chicken stock. Reduce the heat to medium and simmer for 20 minutes to combine all flavors. Add the cilantro. Taste and adjust the seasonings. Serve the soup in bowls, garnished with basil chiffonade and a hearty dollop of sour cream.

Silky Fennel Soup with Alaskan King Crab

Fennel is often compared to anise, but it has a far sweeter, more delicate flavor. When shopping for fennel, look for bulbs with the greens still attached. The greens will show age much sooner than the bulb. The bulb itself should be heavy and firm. Do not worry if it has some slight signs of browning.

Yield: 12 cups, 8 servings

5 fennel bulbs (about 5 pounds)
2½ tablespoons olive oil
1 yellow onion, diced
1 pound Yukon Gold potatoes, peeled and diced
1 tablespoon Pernod (anise-flavored liqueur)
8 cups rich chicken stock
1 teaspoon kosher salt
1 teaspoon freshly ground pepper
1 pound Alaskan king crabmeat

Trim the fennel down to the bulbs, reserving 8 fronds. Halve the bulbs lengthwise, core, and slice thinly. Set aside.

In a large, heavy-bottomed stockpot, heat the oil over medium-high heat. Add the onion and sauté until golden. Add the fennel and potatoes. Turn to coat completely with oil. Sauté for 5 minutes. Deglaze the pan with the Pernod. Add the chicken stock and bring to a boil. Reduce the heat and simmer for 25 minutes. When the potatoes and fennel are very tender, purée the soup. Season with salt and pepper. Taste and adjust the seasonings.

Carefully pick over the crab to remove any shell fragments. Divide the crab among the serving bowls. Ladle the soup on top of the crab. Serve garnished with the reserved fennel fronds.

Mexican Butternut Squash Bisque

This soup makes a very nice first course for any Mexican-style meal. Cooking the squash with the milk and cream allows the squash flavor to permeate the soup.

Yield: 12 cups, 8 servings

Soup
1 butternut squash, about 3 pounds
4 tablespoons butter, divided
¼ cup maple syrup
1 cup whole milk
½ cup heavy cream
1 red onion, diced
1 tablespoon minced garlic
2 teaspoons dark chili powder
2 teaspoons ground cumin
½ teaspoon ground cinnamon
1 teaspoon kosher salt
1 whole canned chipotle chile
1 teaspoon adobo sauce
1 cup flat light beer
6 cups rich chicken stock, divided
¼ cup fresh lime juice
1 cup chopped fresh cilantro

Toppings
½ cup sour cream
¼ cup heavy cream
1 cup Hot and Spicy Pumpkin Seeds (recipe follows)

To make the soup: Preheat the oven to 375°F. Wash the squash and cut it in half lengthwise. Remove and discard the seeds and membrane. Generously butter a casserole dish, using 2 tablespoons of the butter. Place the squash, cut sides down, in the dish. Add the maple syrup, milk, and cream. Cover with foil and bake for 25 minutes. When the squash is very tender, remove it from the oven, remove the foil, and allow to cool. Pour the cream mixture into a container and set aside. When cool enough to handle, scoop the pulp from the squash and set aside.

In a large, heavy-bottomed stockpot, melt the remaining 2 tablespoons butter over medium-high heat. Add the onion and garlic, and sauté until golden. Add the chili powder, cumin, cinnamon, and salt, stirring to coat with the onion mixture. Add the chipotle chile and adobo sauce. Deglaze the pot with the beer, and simmer for 5 minutes. Reduce the heat and add 3 cups of the chicken stock. Add the reserved squash pulp, and mix well. Slowly stir in the reserved cream mixture. Purée the soup in the pot with a handheld blender. Continue adding stock until the desired consistency is reached. Taste and adjust the seasonings, and remove from the heat. Add lime juice and cilantro to taste.

Toppings: Mix the sour cream and heavy cream together. Drizzle over the soup as it is served, and garnish with Hot and Spicy Pumpkin Seeds.

Hot and Spicy Pumpkin Seeds

Use as a garnish for Mexican Butternut Squash Bisque. Make a double batch of these seeds and eat them as a zesty snack.

Yield: 1 cup

½ teaspoon garlic salt
½ teaspoon ground cumin
1 teaspoon dark chili powder
¼ teaspoon cayenne
1 teaspoon dried cilantro
1 tablespoon butter
1 cup hulled raw pumpkin seeds

In a small bowl, mix together the salt, cumin, chili powder, cayenne, and cilantro. In a heavy-bottomed skillet, preferably cast iron, melt the butter over medium-high heat. When the butter is slightly browned, add the pumpkin seeds. Stir to coat with the butter. Add the spices and continue to stir. Reduce the heat to medium, continuing to stir. Sauté until the pumpkin seeds start to pop. Cool the seeds on a paper towel. When cool, store in an airtight container.

Cold Corn Chowder with Ruby Radishes and Grilled Shrimp

Use only fresh corn for this late-summer favorite. When buying corn, look for ears with bright green, tight-fitting husks and golden-brown silk. The peppery flavor of the radishes highlights the sweetness of the corn. Because this soup is chilled, you can prepare it a day in advance.

Yield: 12 cups, 8 servings

3 ears white corn
3 ears yellow corn
10 cups whole milk
3 chicken bouillon cubes
1 tablespoon butter
¾ cup diced red onion
½ cup diced celery
½ teaspoon ground nutmeg
1 teaspoon kosher salt
½ teaspoon ground white pepper
⅛ teaspoon cayenne
½ cup dry white wine
¼ cup chopped fresh thyme
20 large shrimp
1 tablespoon olive oil
½ cup chopped fresh chives
1 cup grated ruby red radishes

Shuck the corn. Bring a large pot of water to a boil. Add the corn and return to a boil. Once it returns to a boil, let the corn cook for 4 to 5 minutes. Drain, reserving 1 cup of the corn water. Rinse the corn under cold running water until cool enough to handle. Using a small knife, scrape the kernels from the ears. Transfer the kernels to a medium bowl. Place the cobs back in the empty stockpot, add the milk, and bring to a simmer. Crush the bouillon cubes in the reserved corn water, add to the milk, and continue to simmer.

In a large skillet over medium-high heat, melt the butter. When slightly browned, add the onion and celery, and sauté for 3 minutes. Add the nutmeg, salt, white pepper, and cayenne. Deglaze the pan with the white wine. Remove from the heat and add to the corn milk. Remove the cobs from the milk, squeezing them first to get all the flavor into the liquid. Add half of the reserved corn and purée the soup in the pot with a handheld blender. Add the thyme, remove from the heat, and let cool. When cool, stir in the rest of the corn. Refrigerate for 4 hours before serving.

To serve: Over medium-high heat, preheat a ridged grill pan. Peel and devein the shrimp, leaving the tails on. Lightly coat the grill pan with the oil. Grill the shrimp for 2 minutes on each side. Set 2 shrimp in the center of each bowl. Ladle chilled soup over the shrimp. Garnish with the chives and radishes.

Provençal White Bean Soup

This is a high-protein, low-fat soup with incredible flavor. Serve it as an easy entrée with a loaf of good, crusty French bread.

Yield: 10 cups, 6 servings

2 tablespoons olive oil
½ cup minced shallots
¼ cup minced garlic
¼ cup chopped fresh rosemary
¼ cup grated lemon zest
1½ teaspoons kosher salt
1 teaspoon freshly ground pepper
1 (28-ounce) can diced tomatoes in juice
1½ cups cooked white beans, rinsed well and drained
5 cups rich chicken stock
2 bunches fresh arugula, rinsed well, drained, and torn

In a large, heavy-bottomed stockpot, heat the oil over medium-high heat. Add the shallots and garlic. Sauté until slightly golden. Reduce the heat to medium. Add the rosemary and lemon zest, and season with the salt and pepper. Add the diced tomatoes and their juice. Simmer until the liquid has reduced by half. Add the white beans and chicken stock. Simmer, uncovered, for 30 minutes, stirring occasionally. Set out the desired number of bowls. Place some torn arugula in the bottom of each bowl. Ladle the soup on top and serve.

Salads

The short, cool growing season of our mountainous region of Interior Alaska has challenged our gardening savvy. Today we not only utilize cold frames and raised beds, we also have a commercial-size greenhouse and compost bins heated by waste heat from the generators that produce our electricity. Succession planting, both in the greenhouse and outdoors, provides the kitchens of Camp Denali and North Face Lodge with a steady supply of leafy greens, herbs, and edible flowers throughout the season. By mid-summer we add greenhouse-grown tomatoes and cucumbers.

Lettuces and Salad Greens

Green salads have come a long way from iceberg lettuce with ranch dressing. Today's lettuces and salad greens range from fragile, tender varieties to those that are heartier and more robust. Some are delicately flavored, while others lend a slightly bitter or peppery component.

Arugula

The tender green leaves of arugula, also known as rocket, are mildly peppery. Try to buy arugula with the roots still attached; this will keep the leaves fresher longer. Arugula is an excellent source of vitamins A and C.

Belgian Endive

Crisp and crunchy, the tightly packed, cream-colored leaves of Belgian endive are slightly bitter. The leaves of these tight bundles should be cut away from the core, rather than torn, because they are so fleshy and tend to bruise easily.

Bok Choy

Bok choy is a mild, versatile vegetable often referred to as Chinese cabbage. It has crunchy white stalks with tender, dark green leaves. Also available is baby bok choy, which has a sweeter, more delicate flavor than the larger variety.

Butterhead Lettuce

The heads of butterhead lettuce are small, round, and loose leafed with a rich, sweet flavor. Boston and Bibb are the most common varieties.

Frisée

A member of the chicory family, frisée has delicately slender, curly leaves. It has a mildly bitter flavor and ranges in color from yellowish white to pale green. Select frisée with crisp leaves and no signs of wilting.

Mesclun Greens

Mesclun is a combination of young, small salad greens. The mix can vary, depending on the source. It usually includes oak leaf lettuce, sorrel, frisée, radicchio, and arugula.

Radicchio

Radicchio is the best-known member of the chicory family. The tight heads range in color from a deep magenta red to a dark purple, with predominantly white ribs. Its flavor is much milder than that of other chicories, and it is excellent when lightly grilled.

Romaine

Crunchy, crisp romaine lettuce has a slightly earthy flavor. The outer leaves are dark green, while the inner ones are a much paler celadon. The integrity of this lettuce makes it essential in Caesar salads because it can stand up to its thick, creamy dressing.

Spinach

Many markets now carry baby spinach in bulk, making it the best option for spinach salads. If baby spinach is not available, look for bunches of flat-leaf spinach rather than the curly-leaf variety. The latter is fine for cooking but is rather fibrous in its raw form.

Oils

One can easily be overwhelmed by the huge variety of available oils. Following are brief descriptions of the oils most commonly used for salads. Experiment to find out which flavors appeal to you.

Almond Oil

Almond oil is obtained by pressing sweet almonds. It has the delicate flavor and aroma of lightly toasted almonds and ranges in color from very light gold to dark brown. The dark-colored oil generally has a richer, truer flavor.

Canola Oil

Canola oil is the most commonly used oil in the United States. It is actually oil pressed from the rapeseed, but the name was changed for marketability. It is very pale in color and has an extremely bland flavor. This oil works well in salad dressings where the flavor base comes from the vinegar or seasonings.

Chile Oil

Chile oil is made by steeping hot red chiles in vegetable oil for 12 hours to release their heat and flavor. The oil picks up a delicate reddish color from the chiles. A mainstay in Asian cooking, this oil, used sparingly, adds a subtle heat to any salad dressing.

Citrus Oils

Citrus oils are extracted from the rinds of citrus fruits. They tend to be thin in consistency but have a very bold, strong flavor. Only a few drops will carry a strong citrus tang throughout any salad.

Corn Oil

Obtained from the endosperm of corn kernels, corn oil has little flavor or odor. It works well in egg-based salad dressings and homemade mayonnaise.

Extra-Virgin Olive Oil

Extra-virgin olive oil is the oil obtained from the first pressing of olives. It has very low acidity, a distinctive fruity flavor, and can range in color from pale champagne to bright green.

Grapeseed Oil

The slight grape flavor retained in grapeseed oil, which is extracted from grape seeds, subtly enhances any wine-based vinaigrette.

Hazelnut Oil

Hazelnut oil is a fragrant, full-flavored oil that is cold-pressed from hazelnuts and tastes strongly of the toasted nut. It is best used to finish a salad or blended with a lighter oil.

Herb Oil

You can make your own herb-infused oil and use it to finish a salad or drizzle around the edge of a plate for an elegant garnish. Simply steep herbs in a blend of vegetable and olive oil for 5 hours, then pour it through a strainer lined with a coffee filter. For best color and flavor, use a blend of dried and fresh herbs.

Mustard Oil

An extremely strong, hot, pungent oil, mustard oil is made from cold-pressed mustard seeds blended with canola oil. When added to a marinade, it adds a spicy, even heat. Blend with a milder oil for a zesty salad dressing.

Olive Oil

Olive oil is a highly acclaimed, commonly used oil obtained by cold-pressing tree-ripened olives. Cold pressing is a chemical-free process in which the fruit or seeds are pressed repeatedly to extract their oil. The oil can vary dramatically in color, flavor, and aroma due to differences in crop and climate conditions. This is a great base oil with limitless culinary applications. (See also Extra-Virgin Olive Oil.)

Safflower Oil

Safflower oil is favored for salad dressings because it does not solidify when chilled. It is remarkably flavorless and colorless. It is not as nutritionally beneficial as other oils due to the absence of vitamin E.

Sesame Oil

There are two basic types of sesame oil. One is lighter in color and has a delicate flavor for use in salads. The darker oil, often referred to as Asian sesame oil, has a strong flavor and should be used to accent marinades and dressings. When blended with a lighter oil, it retains a bold flavor but is not overwhelming.

Vinegars

Most salad dressings and vinaigrettes are made by blending an oil with an acid. The primary acid used is vinegar. As with oils, a huge variety of vinegars is available in most markets, differing greatly in acidity and flavor. Here are some brief descriptions of the most commonly used vinegars.

Balsamic Vinegar

Balsamic vinegar is rich, sweet, and earthy. It originally hailed from Italy but is now made domestically as well. Made from Trebbiano grape juice, it is transferred from one wooden cask to another as it ages, allowing the flavor to be enhanced by the different woods used to make the barrels. Shop for quality in balsamic vinegar, even if it costs a bit more. Many of the cheaper ones are just red wine vinegar with caramel coloring added.

Champagne and Wine Vinegars

Red wine vinegar is the most common wine vinegar, with a clean, sharp flavor. White wine vinegar has a higher acidity and can be rather pungent. Champagne vinegar is the most subtle and the sweetest of all the wine vinegars.

Cider Vinegar

One of the most commonly used vinegars, cider vinegar is a staple in most kitchens. It has the very rich, fruity flavor of fermented cider, with a delicate acid base.

Fruit-Infused Vinegars

Vinegars infused with fruit are great in salads and can offer a subtle sweetness to a simple vinegar. You can make them by steeping fruit in vinegar and then straining out the fruit. When using citrus, steep the rind only. If the vinegar appears cloudy, strain it through a coffee filter.

Herb-Infused Vinegars

Herb vinegars work best when a true herb flavor is desired throughout a salad. They consist of herbs steeped in a mild vinegar, such as rice wine vinegar. The stronger the herb, the more flavor will be imparted to the vinegar. Rosemary and tarragon work wonderfully.

Malt Vinegar

Malt vinegar, popular in Great Britain, is derived from malted barley. It has a mild flavor and pairs wonderfully with nuts, bitter greens, and tart apples.

Rice Wine Vinegar

Rice wine vinegar is a very clear vinegar. It is extremely mild and has relatively low acidity. This vinegar works well when paired with citrus juices.

Sherry Vinegar

Originally from Spain, sherry vinegar is a nutty, rich, oaky vinegar similar to balsamic vinegar. Both are aged in oak casks.

Mixed Field Greens with Mustard Chive Dressing

You can use any combination of lettuces in this simple salad. Chive flowers make it an elegant starter for any meal.

Yield: 8 servings

1 small head butter lettuce
1 small head red oak leaf lettuce
1 bunch arugula
2 teaspoons Dijon mustard
2 teaspoons coarse-grained mustard
2 tablespoons champagne vinegar
1 teaspoon honey
6 tablespoons extra virgin olive oil
1 tablespoon chopped fresh chives
1 teaspoon kosher salt
1 teaspoon freshly ground pepper
1 cup chive flowers

Wash and dry the butter and red oak lettuces and arugula. Gently tear the larger leaves. Toss together in a large salad bowl. Set aside.

In a small bowl, combine the Dijon and coarse-grained mustards, vinegar, and honey. Slowly drizzle in the oil, whisking constantly. Whisk in the chopped chives. Season with the salt and pepper. Taste and adjust the seasonings. Toss the washed lettuce with the dressing, and garnish with the chive flowers.

Carrot Ginger Salad

We serve this in late summer, when sweet, crisp Alaskan carrots are abundant. If using store-bought carrots, make sure they are bright in color and very firm. Try garnishing this salad with chive oil drizzled around the edge of the plate.

Yield: 8 servings

8 medium carrots, trimmed and peeled
1 teaspoon minced garlic
2 tablespoons grated fresh ginger
¼ cup extra-virgin olive oil
1 teaspoon kosher salt
1 teaspoon freshly ground pepper
8 large radicchio leaves

Using a coarse grater, shred the carrots into a large bowl. Mix in the garlic, ginger, olive oil, salt, and pepper. Stir well to combine. Taste and adjust the seasonings. Cover and let stand for 20 minutes, and then strain off any extra liquid. Serve a dollop on each of the radicchio leaves.

Classic Caesar Salad with Parmesan Tuiles

Although first invented in Tijuana in the 1920s, this salad has become an American institution. It is important to use the best ingredients to achieve a truly satisfying flavor.

Yield: 6 servings

1 teaspoon freshly pressed garlic
3 high-quality anchovy fillets
2 tablespoons fresh lemon juice
½ teaspoon balsamic vinegar
¼ teaspoon Worcestershire sauce
1 tablespoon finely grated Parmesan cheese
1 egg, coddled
⅓ cup olive oil
Salt and freshly ground pepper
2 heads romaine lettuce
½ cup homemade croutons (see Minted Pea Soup, page 97)
6 Parmesan Tuiles (recipe follows)

Note: To coddle an egg, plunge raw egg, whole in shell, into boiling water for 30 seconds. Use immediately.

In the bottom of a large salad bowl, using the tines of a sturdy fork, mash the garlic and anchovies to form a paste. Whisk in the lemon juice, balsamic vinegar, Worcestershire sauce, and Parmesan cheese. Slowly whisk in the coddled egg and, still whisking, slowly incorporate the olive oil. Season with salt and pepper to taste.

Wash the romaine and tear the leaves, removing the spine. Spin dry in a salad spinner. Toss the romaine and croutons with the dressing. Serve on chilled plates, garnished with Parmesan Tuiles and sprinkled with more freshly ground pepper.

Parmesan Tuiles

These crisp, baked cheese curls can be made well in advance. Store in an airtight container for up to 2 weeks at room temperature until ready to use.

1 cup grated Parmesan cheese

Preheat the oven to 375°F. Line a sheet pan with parchment paper. Evenly sprinkle the cheese in a 2-inch-wide strip down the center of the sheet. Bake for 5 minutes, or until the cheese is completely melted and golden brown at the edges. Cool slightly. While the cheese is still warm and pliable, cut it into ½-inch-wide strips. Wrap each strip around the handle of a wooden spoon, creating a spiral shape. Allow them to set for a few minutes. Gently slide each tuile off the handle and repeat with the remaining cheese strips. If the cheese gets too firm while still on the sheet pan, return it to a warm oven for a minute. Serve with Classic Caesar Salad.

Frisée and Grilled Mushroom Salad with Hazelnuts

Grilling the mushrooms for this salad intensifies their flavor.

Yield: 6 servings

⅓ cup hazelnuts
1 teaspoon freshly pressed garlic
2 tablespoons champagne vinegar
½ teaspoon maple syrup
¾ teaspoon kosher salt
1 teaspoon freshly ground pepper
¼ cup olive oil
2 tablespoons hazelnut oil
1 pound exotic fresh mushrooms, such as chanterelles, cremini, or shiitake
2 medium heads frisée
2 teaspoons truffle oil

Preheat the oven to 350°F. Toast the hazelnuts in a shallow pan for 10 minutes. Remove the nuts from the oven, wrap them in a dish towel, and rub to remove their skins. Chop the hazelnuts coarsely, and set aside.

Light a grill or preheat a broiler. In a large salad bowl, combine the garlic, vinegar, maple syrup, salt, and pepper. Whisking continuously, slowly drizzle in the olive and hazelnut oils. Taste and adjust the seasonings.

Clean the mushrooms and thread them onto wooden skewers. Brush them lightly with some of the vinaigrette. Grill or broil the mushrooms for 3 to 5 minutes, turning once to cook them evenly. Remove from the grill when tender. Cut the mushrooms into ¼-inch-thick slices. Add to the bowl with the vinaigrette.

Trim and tear the frisée into bite-sized pieces. Toss it in the vinaigrette with the mushrooms, and then toss in the hazelnuts. Serve on chilled plates, drizzled with truffle oil.

Warm Potato Leek Salad with Pistou

*This traditional salad is warm and welcoming when the cooler weather arrives.
At the same time, the heavy dose of basil reminds you of the splendor of summer.*

Yield: 8 servings

6 medium red potatoes, unpeeled
4 leeks, white and pale green parts only
6 tablespoons olive oil, divided
1 teaspoon kosher salt, divided
3 tablespoons Pistou (recipe follows)
1 teaspoon freshly ground pepper
2 tablespoons chiffonade (thin strips) of fresh basil

Wash and boil the potatoes in lightly salted water until tender. Drain and cool.
Cut into 1-inch cubes, leaving on the skin.

Wash the leeks well, trim, and cut into ½-inch lengths. In a medium-size saucepan,
heat 3 tablespoons of the olive oil. Add the leeks and season lightly with some of
the salt. Sauté over medium-high heat for 5 minutes. The leeks should be soft and silky.
In a large bowl, mix together the potatoes and leeks.

In a small saucepan, combine the remaining 3 tablespoons oil with the Pistou and
warm over medium heat. Pour over the potatoes and leeks. Season with remaining
salt and pepper. Serve garnished with basil chiffonade.

Pistou

This is the French version of the classic Italian pesto. It is best to make it in summer when basil is abundant and the flavor is at its peak. Pistou freezes well, so you can be sure to savor the flavors of summer all winter long.

Yield: 1½ cups

1 tablespoon minced garlic
2 teaspoons kosher salt
½ teaspoon freshly ground pepper
2 tablespoons pine nuts
1 cup packed fresh basil leaves
⅔ cup grated Parmesan cheese
¾ cup extra virgin olive oil

Using a food processor, purée together the garlic and salt to form a paste. Add the pine nuts, basil, and cheese. Purée to form a paste. Slowly incorporate the oil. Purée until well blended. Use 3 tablespoons as a dressing for Warm Potato Leek Salad, saving the rest for another use.

Spinach Salad with Roasted Pears and Sugared Pecans

Although pears are available year-round, this salad is best in early autumn, when pears are at their flavor peak. To make this salad a main course, add Roquefort cheese. The salty richness of the cheese pairs well with the sweetness of the pears.

Yield: 8 servings

3 ripe Bartlett pears
1 pound bunch baby spinach leaves with stems removed
1 tablespoon minced shallots
2 tablespoons champagne vinegar
2 tablespoons apple cider
1 tablespoon honey
1 tablespoon honey mustard
1 teaspoon kosher salt
1 teaspoon freshly ground pepper
1 cup olive oil
1 cup Sugared Pecans (recipe follows)

Preheat the oven to 375°F. Wash, core, and slice each of the pears into 12 sections. Set the pear slices on a baking sheet. Roast for 10 to 12 minutes, removing them from the oven when they are just beginning to color. Set aside to cool.

Wash and spin dry the spinach leaves. In a large bowl, combine the shallots, vinegar, cider, honey, mustard, salt, and pepper. Slowly whisk in the olive oil.

Gently toss the spinach with dressing to coat. Arrange the pears on the desired number of plates. Top with dressed spinach, and garnish with 1 cup of Sugared Pecans.

Sugared Pecans

These are great as a salad garnish or on their own as a snack.

Yield: 2 cups

2 cups pecan halves
2 tablespoons honey
2 tablespoons vegetable oil
2 tablespoons water
½ cup sugar
1 tablespoon kosher salt
½ teaspoon cayenne

Preheat the oven to 375°F. Spread the pecan halves on a rimmed baking sheet. Toast for 10 to 12 minutes. They should be very fragrant. Remove from the oven and set aside to cool.

In a small saucepan over medium heat, combine the honey, oil, and water. Bring to a boil, reduce the heat, and add the pecans. Stir together until all of the liquid is absorbed. In a separate bowl, combine the sugar, salt, and cayenne. Mix in the pecans, stirring to coat. Spread out the sugared pecans on parchment paper, and allow to cool completely. Store in an airtight container. Use 1 cup as a garnish for Spinach Salad with Roasted Pears.

Tabbouleh

This Middle Eastern delight is a healthy and refreshing summer salad. We serve it at the height of summer when our greenhouse is overflowing with parsley and the golden and cherry tomatoes are sweet and juicy. It is very important that the herbs in this salad be chopped by hand with a very sharp knife. This keeps their true flavor. A food processor tends to bruise and mash herbs rather than chop them.

Yield: 8 servings

½ cup fine-grain bulgur wheat
⅓ cup fresh lemon juice, divided
1 tablespoon sugar
⅓ cup extra-virgin olive oil
2 teaspoons kosher salt
1 teaspoon freshly ground pepper
⅛ teaspoon cayenne
2 cups chopped fresh parsley
10 cherry tomatoes, halved
10 golden teardrop tomatoes, halved
4 whole scallions, minced
2 tablespoons chopped lemon-mint leaves

Rinse the bulgur under warm running water for 2 minutes; drain well. In a medium bowl, combine the bulgur with ¼ cup of the lemon juice. Set aside until the grains are fluffy, about 30 minutes, depending on the type and age of the grain.

In a separate bowl, combine the remaining lemon juice, sugar, olive oil, salt, pepper, and cayenne. Mix until well incorporated, and set aside.

Add the parsley, cherry and golden tomatoes, scallions, and mint to the bulgur, and toss well to combine. Mix in the dressing, and toss to combine. Cover and refrigerate for 1 to 2 hours to allow the flavors to blend.

Green Bean, Arugula, and Tomato Salad

Five-spice powder can be found in most markets, in the Asian foods section or with the dried spices. You can also create your own using star anise, fennel, cloves, cinnamon, and Sichuan pepper. Although you can make up the components for this salad ahead of time, once it is all mixed together it should be served right away. If left too long, the ginger can overpower the subtle sweetness of the tomatoes.

Yield: 6 servings

1 tablespoon freshly squeezed orange juice
1 tablespoon orange juice concentrate
2 teaspoons soy sauce
1 teaspoon five-spice powder
1 teaspoon minced fresh ginger
1 teaspoon honey
⅓ cup olive oil
⅛ teaspoon red pepper flakes
¼ pound green beans
1½ pounds vine-ripe tomatoes
1 bunch arugula
1 bunch fresh cilantro, chopped

In a small bowl, combine the orange juice, juice concentrate, soy sauce, five-spice powder, ginger, and honey. Whisk together. Slowly incorporate the oil. Season with the red pepper flakes and set aside.

Trim the ends from the beans. Bring a pot of water to a boil over medium-high heat, and cook the beans until crisp-tender. Drain the beans and rinse under cold running water until cool to the touch; set aside.

Slice the tomatoes in half, and cut each half into 6 chunks; set aside. Clean the arugula well, removing all stems. In a large bowl, mix together the arugula, tomatoes, beans, and cilantro. Add the dressing, tossing well to coat. Serve immediately.

Breads

Nothing is more welcoming than the aroma of freshly baked bread from our bakery. Our flours and grains are organic, shipped once a year by barge and truck from a natural foods wholesaler in Seattle. We recommend organic flour because it absorbs less water than nonorganic, commercially milled flour. More essential vitamins are retained and breads have a lighter, chewier texture.

The following are just a few of our favorite recipes, scaled down for home use. Although all recipes are written to be prepared in an electric mixer, they can also be made by hand with a little more elbow grease. Incorporate all the ingredients except flour, with a sturdy spatula or wooden spoon. Mix in flour until a soft dough forms. Then roll up your sleeves and tenderly knead in the remaining flour.

Focaccia

A true Italian focaccia should have a soft, chewy texture with a light, crisp crust. The topping should complement the bread rather than overpower it.

Yield: One 12-by-16-inch sheet or two 10-inch rounds

1½ cups warm water
1 teaspoon sugar
2 teaspoons active dry yeast
4½ cups all-purpose flour, divided
2 teaspoons kosher salt
3 tablespoons olive oil
Topping (recipe follows)

In a small bowl, combine the water and sugar. Using a rubber spatula, mix in the yeast. Allow the yeast to dissolve and become frothy.

In the bowl of an electric mixer fitted with the dough hook, combine 3 cups of the flour and the salt. Make a well in the center, and add the yeast mixture and oil to the well. Mix on low speed until thoroughly incorporated. Continue mixing, adding the remaining flour as needed to form a smooth, soft, elastic dough. This may take up to 10 minutes. Turn the dough out into an oiled bowl, and turn to coat it with oil. Cover and let rise in a warm place until almost doubled in volume.

Gently punch down the dough and turn it out onto a lightly floured work surface. Divide into the desired portions. Roll the dough out to fit the pan or pans you will be using. Lightly coat the pans with oil, and then place the dough on the pans. Cover with the topping. Cover loosely and let rise in a warm place until almost doubled in volume.

Preheat the oven to 400°F. Bake the focaccia until crisp and golden, 20 to 25 minutes. Transfer to a cooling rack to cool.

Topping for Focaccia

The topping we give here is merely a suggestion. Any herbs taste great on this bread, and you can also experiment with olives or Parmesan cheese.

Yield: Enough for 1 recipe of Focaccia

3 tablespoons olive oil
1 cup julienned red onion
Sea salt
Freshly cracked pepper
16 fresh sage leaves

In a large skillet, heat the oil over medium-high heat. Add the onions and sauté until golden. Remove from the heat, and season with salt and pepper. Arrange the sage leaves on top of the rising dough. Top with the sautéed onions. Continue as directed for Focaccia.

Honey Curry Bread

This rich, flavorful bread complements even the simplest dinners.

Yield: Two 1½-pound braids

⅓ cup warm water
2 teaspoons active dry yeast
4 tablespoons butter
1½ tablespoons curry powder
6 tablespoons honey
5 cups all-purpose flour, divided
1 teaspoon kosher salt
1⅓ cups buttermilk
1 egg
1 tablespoon water

In the bowl of an electric mixer fitted with the dough hook, combine the water and yeast. In a small saucepan over medium heat, melt the butter. Add the curry powder and honey. Reduce the heat and cook for 1 minute. Cool to lukewarm. Stir the butter into the yeast water, and let the mixture rest for 1 minute. With the mixer on low speed, slowly incorporate 2½ cups of the flour, and mix for 5 minutes. This allows the gluten to develop. Add the salt and then slowly add the remaining 2½ cups flour, alternating with the buttermilk, adding enough flour to form a smooth, soft, elastic dough. Turn the dough out into an oiled bowl. Turn the dough to coat it with oil, cover it loosely, and set it in a warm place to rise until almost doubled.

Gently punch down the dough and divide it in half. Divide each half into 3 equal pieces. Roll each of these out to form ropes. Braid 3 ropes together, starting at the middle and working out to each end. Pinch the ends together and tuck them under. Carefully transfer the braid to a sheet pan lined with parchment paper, and repeat with the remaining dough. Cover loosely and let rise in a warm place until almost doubled in volume.

Preheat the oven to 375°F. In a small bowl, whisk together the egg and water to make an egg wash. Brush the braids gently with the egg wash. Bake for 30 minutes, until the bread sounds slightly hollow when tapped and is a deep golden brown. Allow to cool on a cooling rack.

Sourdough Baguettes

Depending on the strength of your starter, this bread can have subtle, sour overtones or a rich, chewy tang. Either way it is simply irresistible fresh from the oven with a little butter.

Yield: 2 long baguettes

1 cup warm water
1½ cups Sourdough Starter (see page 19)
3 tablespoons honey
1 teaspoon active dry yeast
3 cups bread flour
3 tablespoons buttermilk powder
1 tablespoon sour cream
2 teaspoons kosher salt
¼ cup olive oil
2 cups all-purpose flour

In the bowl of an electric mixer, using a rubber spatula to stir, mix together the warm water, Sourdough Starter, honey, and yeast. Let stand for a few minutes, until the yeast is frothy. Fit the mixer with the dough hook. With the mixer on low speed, add the bread flour. Mix for 5 minutes to develop the gluten. Scrape down the sides of the bowl as needed. Mix in the buttermilk powder, sour cream, salt, and olive oil. Combine well. Continue mixing, adding all-purpose flour as needed to form a smooth, soft, elastic dough. Turn out into an oiled bowl, turning the dough to coat it with oil. Cover and let rise in a warm place until almost doubled in volume.

Gently punch down the dough and turn it out onto a lightly floured work surface. Divide the dough into 2 portions. Gently kneading and rolling to push out any air bubbles, shape the dough into baguettes. Carefully transfer the loaves to baguette pans dusted with flour, and cover loosely. Let rise in a warm place until almost doubled.

Preheat the oven to 375°F. Using a very sharp knife, gently slash the top of each baguette, making 3 cuts about ¼ inch deep. Place a shallow baking dish filled with 1 inch of boiling water at the base of your oven. Bake the baguettes for 30 minutes, until they sound slightly hollow when tapped. Allow to cool slightly on a cooling rack before serving.

Russian Black Bread

Similar to traditional pumpernickel bread, this bread has a more intense flavor. It's rich mocha color is due to the addition of coffee and cocoa.

Yield: 2 round loaves

2 cups warm water
¼ cup honey
1 tablespoon molasses
2 teaspoons active dry yeast
1 tablespoon instant coffee granules
2 cups rye flour
2 cups bread flour
¼ cup unsweetened cocoa powder
2 teaspoons crushed caraway seeds
1 teaspoon crushed fennel seeds
1 tablespoon kosher salt
¼ cup vegetable oil
2 cups all-purpose flour
1 egg white
1 tablespoon milk

In the bowl of an electric mixer, using a rubber spatula to stir, mix together the warm water, honey, molasses, and yeast. Let stand for a few minutes, until the yeast is foamy. Fit the mixer with the dough hook. With the mixer on low speed, add the coffee granules, rye flour, bread flour, cocoa powder, and caraway and fennel seeds. Mix for 5 minutes to develop the gluten. Scrape down the sides of the bowl as needed. Mix in the salt and vegetable oil. Continue mixing, adding the all-purpose flour as needed to form a smooth, soft, elastic dough. Turn out into an oiled bowl, turning the dough to coat it with oil. Cover and let rise in a warm place until almost doubled in volume.

Gently punch down the dough and turn it out onto a lightly floured work surface. Divide the dough into 2 portions. Gently kneading and rolling, shape the dough into 2 rounded mounds. Set each mound into a lightly greased 9-inch cake or pie tin. Cover loosely and let rise in a warm place until almost doubled in volume.

Preheat the oven to 350°F. In a small bowl, whisk together the egg white and milk to make an egg wash. Using a very sharp knife, slash an X into the tops of the rounds, making cuts ¼ inch deep. Brush the bread gently with the egg wash. Bake for 45 minutes, until the bread sounds slightly hollow when tapped. Allow to cool on a cooling rack.

Orange Rye Rolls

The success of these zesty rolls is in the rising. They should feel very light and puffy before baking.

Yield: 3 dozen rolls

1¼ cups warm water
¼ cup honey
3 tablespoons molasses
2 tablespoons active dry yeast
¾ cup orange juice concentrate
1 tablespoon grated orange zest
1½ cups rye flour
1 cup whole wheat flour
6 tablespoons butter, melted
2 eggs
¾ teaspoon baking soda
1 teaspoon kosher salt
3½ cups all-purpose flour
1 egg white
1 tablespoon milk

In the bowl of an electric mixer, using a spatula to stir, mix together the warm water, honey, molasses, and yeast. Let stand for a few minutes, until the yeast is foamy. Mix in the orange juice concentrate and orange zest. Fit the mixer with the dough hook. With the mixer on low speed, add the rye and wheat flours. Mix for 5 minutes to develop the gluten. Scrape down the sides of the bowl as needed. Mix in the butter, eggs, baking soda, and salt. Continue mixing, adding the all-purpose flour as needed to form a smooth, soft, elastic dough. Turn out into an oiled bowl, turning the dough to coat it with oil. Cover and let rise in a warm place until almost doubled in volume.

Gently punch down the dough and turn it out onto a lightly floured work surface. Divide the dough into 3 equal pieces. Roll out each piece into a long rope. Cut each rope into 12 pieces. Gently form each piece into the desired shape. Set on a sheet pan lined with parchment paper. Cover loosely and let rise in a warm place until almost doubled in volume.

Preheat the oven to 350°F. In a small bowl, whisk together the egg white and milk to make an egg wash. Gently brush the tops of the rolls with the egg wash. Bake for 20 to 25 minutes. Allow to cool slightly on a cooling rack before serving.

Long-Rise French Bread

Don't worry if this dough is loose and sticky. The high water content and long rise time give this bread a wonderfully chewy texture and a crisp crust. The dough will retain its shape and bake evenly if you bake it in a baguette pan rather than on a sheet pan.

Yield: 2 long baguettes

2 cups warm water
1 teaspoon honey
2 teaspoons active dry yeast
6½ cups bread flour
2 teaspoons kosher salt
2 tablespoons coarse cornmeal

In the bowl of an electric mixer, using a rubber spatula to stir, mix together the warm water, honey, and yeast. Let stand for a few minutes, until the yeast is foamy. Fit the mixer with the dough hook. With the mixer on low speed, slowly incorporate the flour. Continue mixing on the lowest speed for 10 minutes. This helps develop the gluten. Mix in the salt. Turn out into an oiled bowl, turning the dough to coat it with oil. Cover loosely and let rise in a cool place for a minimum of 3 hours, until almost tripled in volume.

Gently punch down the dough and turn it onto a lightly floured work surface. Divide the dough into 2 pieces. Gently kneading and rolling, shape the dough into baguettes. Dust baguette pans generously with the cornmeal. Set the loaves in the pans, cover loosely, and let rise in a cool place until almost doubled in volume.

Preheat the oven to 450°F. Using a very sharp knife, gently slash the top of each baguette 3 times, making cuts about ¼ inch deep. Place a shallow baking dish filled with 1 inch of boiling water at the base of your oven. Bake the baguettes for 15 to 20 minutes, until the tops are golden brown and the bread sounds slightly hollow when tapped. Cool slightly on a cooling rack before serving.

Entrées

After hors d'oeuvres, guests are invited into the dining rooms, gathering around large tables with friends and family. Dinner is served family style, with a special menu featured each evening. We begin with the freshest fish, finest cuts of meat, and highest-quality vegetables, preparing and presenting the food with simple elegance.

Lamb

Lamb meat has a rich red color and delicate marbling, similar to beef but with a much more distinctive flavor. The most prized cut is the rack, the eight-rib section (on each side) between the shoulder and the loin cuts. Its mild, refined flavor and fine grain make it our serving choice. True, it is more expensive than other cuts of lamb, but little trimming is required, reducing waste and saving preparation time.

Lamb Chops with Gremolata

Here the rich, savory flavor of lamb is complemented by the fresh, robust, zesty flavor of Gremolata. Round out the menu with White Beans with Tomatoes and Garlic (see page 168). Add a splash of color with lightly sautéed green beans.

Yield: 4 servings

Two 8-rib lamb racks
2 tablespoons kosher salt
2 tablespoons freshly ground pepper
1 cup Gremolata (recipe follows), divided
½ cup olive oil, divided

Trim the lamb and cut it into double-rib portions. Season with the salt and pepper, and set it in a large casserole dish. In a small bowl, combine ½ cup of the Gremolata with ¼ cup of the olive oil. Pour over the seasoned chops and let stand for 30 minutes to infuse the flavors.

Preheat the oven to 300°F. In a large, heavy-bottomed, ovenproof skillet, heat the remaining ¼ cup oil over medium-high heat. When the oil is hot, begin searing the chops, working in batches, if necessary. Sear for a few minutes on each side, until they are caramel colored. The timing depends on the thickness of the chops. At this point, the chops are cooked to medium-rare. If you desire a more well-done chop, cover loosely with foil and transfer to the oven until the desired internal temperature and color are reached. Arrange 2 double-rib chops per plate. Sprinkle with the remaining ½ cup Gremolata.

Gremolata

Gremolata seems to grab the essence of summer in its aroma and flavor. It is best used when fresh. Do not store for longer than a few days, as its zesty, complex flavors tend to combine and get lost if kept any longer.

Yield: 1 cup

1 cup chopped fresh parsley
3 tablespoons minced garlic
3 tablespoons grated lemon zest
2 tablespoons chopped fresh rosemary

In a small container, mix together all ingredients. Store in the refrigerator until ready to use. Serve with Lamb Chops.

Coriander-Crusted Rack of Lamb with Hard Cider Sauce

Coriander and cilantro are derived from the same plant. Coriander refers to the seeds of the plant, while the leaves are often called cilantro. Coriander has a subtle, spicy sweetness and is frequently used in Asian cooking and in curries. Cilantro has a distinctively fresh peppery taste. Grilled radicchio and tangy, sweet Lemon Parsley Orzo Pasta (see page 172) would complement this savory dish.

Yield: 4 servings

Two 8-rib lamb racks
½ cup coriander seeds
½ cup chopped fresh cilantro
2 tablespoons kosher salt
2 tablespoons freshly ground pepper
½ cup olive oil
½ cup dry white wine
Hard Cider Sauce (recipe follows)
1 lemon, quartered and thinly sliced
½ cup pitted, chopped kalamata olives
¼ cup chopped fresh parsley
¼ cup chopped fresh cilantro

Trim the lamb racks to remove any excess fat. In a small skillet over medium heat, toast the coriander seeds for 3 to 4 minutes, shaking the skillet constantly to prevent burning. Spread the seeds out onto a large plate to cool. When cool, use the back of the skillet to crush the seeds. Combine the crushed coriander seeds, cilantro, salt, and pepper on the plate. Roll the lamb in this mixture, pressing to form a crust. Place the lamb in a dish, cover with plastic wrap, and refrigerate for 2 hours to combine flavors.

In a large, heavy-bottomed skillet, heat the oil over medium-high heat. When the oil is hot, sear the lamb racks, crust side down. Adjusting the heat as needed, sauté for 5 minutes. Flip the racks over and sauté for 4 more minutes, or longer if desired. Transfer the lamb to a plate lined with paper towels. Cover loosely with foil to keep it warm.

Return the skillet to high heat and deglaze it with the wine. Add the Hard Cider Sauce, whisking constantly. Reduce the heat and simmer for 2 minutes. Remove from the heat, strain the sauce through a fine sieve, and keep warm.

Carve the prepared racks into chops. Arrange 4 chops on each plate, and top with the sauce. Garnish with the lemon and olives, and sprinkle parsley and cilantro over the plates.

Hard Cider Sauce

This sauce enhances the flavor of lamb with a subtle sweetness.

Yield: 2 cups

4 tablespoons butter
½ cup minced shallots
1 tablespoon minced garlic
3 tablespoons all-purpose flour
1 cup hard cider
2 cups rich lamb stock
Kosher salt
Freshly ground pepper

In a large, heavy-bottomed sauté pan, melt the butter over medium-high heat. Add the shallots and garlic and sauté until golden. Sprinkle the flour on top, whisking constantly. Reduce the heat and continue whisking while cooking for 2 minutes. Slowly whisk in the cider, and return to a simmer. Continue to simmer, whisking constantly, until the cider is reduced by half. Slowly whisk in the lamb stock, and return to a simmer. Simmer, stirring constantly, until the sauce is reduced by half. Season with salt and pepper to taste. Keep warm until ready to serve.

Halibut

Fresh Alaskan halibut is prized for its delicate flavor. When shopping for halibut, look for fillets that are firm and pale, with opaque flesh. Halibut should have almost no odor, other than a light, sweet cucumber scent. If only frozen halibut is available, try our recipe for Sour Cream Halibut in the Camp Denali Classics chapter (page 211).

Herb-Crusted Halibut with Beurre Blanc

The herb coating forms a crust around the halibut, sealing it and delicately steaming the fish. Staying in tune with the classic flavor of Beurre Blanc, we serve this preparation with oven-roasted sweet potatoes and sautéed asparagus.

Yield: 6 servings

2 pounds halibut fillet
2 eggs
2 tablespoons heavy cream
1 teaspoon kosher salt
1 teaspoon freshly ground pepper
2 cups homemade bread crumbs
2 tablespoons chopped fresh oregano
2 tablespoons chopped fresh marjoram
3 tablespoons chopped fresh thyme
3 tablespoons chopped fresh parsley
2 tablespoons butter, melted
Beurre Blanc (recipe follows)

Preheat the oven to 425°F. Cut the halibut fillet into the desired portion size. Pat dry with paper towels.

In a small bowl, whisk together the eggs, cream, salt, and pepper. In a separate larger bowl, mix together the bread crumbs with the oregano, marjoram, thyme, and parsley. Brush a sheet pan with the melted butter. Dip the halibut in the egg/cream mixture, and then coat it thoroughly with the herbed bread crumbs. Set on the prepared sheet pan. Repeat with the remaining halibut.

Bake the halibut for 15 minutes. The time may vary depending on the thickness of the fillets. Divide the Beurre Blanc among the desired number of plates, and set a piece of crusted halibut on top of the sauce on each plate.

Beurre Blanc

This sauce is the definition of simple elegance. The subtle lemon overtones complement the sweetness of halibut. To ensure a smooth sauce that does not separate, keep the sauce around 90 °F.

Yield: 1 cup

½ pound (2 sticks) butter, cubed and softened, divided
1 shallot, minced
1 tablespoon chopped fresh thyme
½ teaspoon kosher salt
¼ teaspoon cayenne
3 tablespoons dry white wine
1 tablespoon cream, scalded

In a saucepan over medium-high heat, melt a small amount of the butter. Add the shallot and sauté until tender. Season with the thyme, salt, and cayenne. Add the wine and simmer until reduced to 1 tablespoon. Reduce the heat and slowly start whisking in half the remaining butter. When you've added half of the butter, whisk in the scalded cream, and then continue whisking in the remaining butter. Remove from the heat, taste, and adjust the seasonings. Keep warm until ready to serve.

Grilled Halibut Steaks with Mango Vinaigrette and Cilantro Pesto

Make the sauces ahead of time for this easy, light, summery dish.

Yield: 6 servings

½ onion
6 halibut steaks, 8 ounces each
5 tablespoons olive oil
1 teaspoon kosher salt
1 teaspoon freshly ground pepper
Mango Vinaigrette (recipe follows)
Cilantro Pesto (recipe follows)

Light a charcoal or gas grill. Secure the onion on the end of a grilling fork. Dip the onion in the oil and rub it on the grill racks to season them. Drizzle the remaining oil over the halibut steaks. Season with the salt and pepper. Grill the halibut steaks for 2 to 3 minutes per side. Serve drizzled with the Mango Vinaigrette and Cilantro Pesto.

Mango Vinaigrette

Try this vinaigrette with chicken or as a salad dressing.

Yield: 1 cup

½ cup mango purée (if not available, purée a very ripe mango with
 some mango nectar)
1 tablespoon fresh lime juice
1 tablespoon minced red onion
1 teaspoon red pepper flakes
1 teaspoon kosher salt
2 teaspoons sugar
2 teaspoons rice wine vinegar
⅓ cup olive oil

In a large bowl, combine the mango purée, lime juice, red onion, red pepper flakes, salt, sugar, and vinegar. Whisk together to fully combine. Slowly whisk in the oil. Taste and adjust the seasonings. Store in the refrigerator until ready to use.

Cilantro Pesto

You can also use this pesto on grilled shrimp.

Yield: 1 cup

1 cup fresh cilantro leaves
1 tablespoon hulled raw pumpkin seeds
1 tablespoon fresh lime juice
2 teaspoons minced garlic
1 teaspoon kosher salt
1 teaspoon freshly ground pepper
5 tablespoons olive oil

Using a food processor, purée together the cilantro, pumpkin seeds, lime juice, and garlic to form a paste. Season with the salt and pepper. Slowly incorporate the oil. Purée until well blended and smooth. Store in the refrigerator until ready to use.

Pork

Pork is a very lean and high-protein alternative to chicken or beef. Because of changes in the raising and butchering of pigs during the past twenty years, the recommended internal temperature for serving pork has been reduced dramatically. The FDA currently states that pork can be served at an internal temperature of 138°F. This is a bit too pink for most palates, so we recommend serving pork at an internal temperature of 150°F. Pork cooked to this temperature will render a tender, juicy cut, but without pink flesh. The following recipes are written for pork tenderloin. There are many different and delicious cuts of pork. You can adapt any of the following recipes to the cut of your choice by altering the cooking time.

Brining

Many meats benefit significantly from brining. Brining is very similar to marinating, but is not quite so overpowering. It enhances the meat's natural flavor, adding moisture and subtle seasoning.

A basic brine is made of 1 cup kosher salt to 1 gallon water. When you brine meat, it absorbs the saltwater. The salt in the brine denatures the meat's proteins, causing them to unwind and form a matrix that traps the water. Some brines include garlic, sugar, spices, and seasonings; those flavors get trapped in the meat, too. Brining can carry flavor throughout the meat rather than just coating the surface. Adding sugar can balance the salt with sweetness and aid in the browning of the meat when cooked.

The recommended brines depend a great deal on the type of meat you are brining, as well as on the ultimate flavor you hope to achieve. Brining times also vary depending on the type and cut of meat. If meat is left too long in a brine or the brine is too strong, the meat will have a salty flavor and a mushy, unappealing texture. Experiment to find out what type and strength of brine you prefer.

Basic Brine for Pork Tenderloin

Always make sure there is enough brine to completely cover the meat. Weigh down the meat, if necessary, to keep it from floating.

Yield: 4 cups

4 cups water
¼ cup kosher salt
¼ cup maple syrup
¼ cup brown sugar
1 clove garlic, sliced
2 sprigs rosemary
3 sprigs thyme
1 bay leaf
1 teaspoon anise or fennel seeds
1 tablespoon juniper berries

In a large stockpot over medium-high heat, bring the water to a boil. Add the salt, maple syrup, and brown sugar. Reduce the heat and simmer until the sugar and salt are completely dissolved. Remove from the heat. Add the garlic, rosemary, thyme, bay leaf, anise or fennel seeds, and juniper berries. Cool completely. When cool, transfer to a noncorrosive container. Add the meat to the brine and refrigerate for 12 to 14 hours.

Grilled Pork Tenderloin with Caramelized Apples and Maple Mustard Sauce

This dish has a decidedly autumn flair. Grilling caramelizes the sugar infused into the pork from the brine, giving it great flavor and color. We serve this pork tenderloin entrée over wilted greens or lightly dressed spinach with Wild Rice Cakes (see page 170).

Yield: 6 servings

Caramelized Apples
2 medium Granny Smith apples
2 tablespoons butter, melted
1 teaspoon kosher salt
1 teaspoon freshly ground pepper
¼ cup dried cranberries

Pork
2 pork tenderloins, 12 ounces each, brined (see Basic Brine recipe, page 139)
¼ cup olive oil
2 teaspoons freshly ground pepper
2 tablespoons chopped fresh rosemary
2 tablespoons maple syrup
1 tablespoon Dijon mustard
1 cup Maple Mustard Sauce (recipe follows)
6 small sprigs rosemary

To caramelize the apples: Preheat the oven to 400°F. Peel, core, and slice each apple into 12 wedges. Toss the slices in the melted butter, and season with salt and pepper. Spread the apple slices on a sheet pan, and bake for 12 minutes, until slightly golden. Remove from the oven and transfer to a medium bowl. Toss together with the dried cranberries, and set aside.

To grill the pork: Light a grill. Remove the tenderloins from the brine. Rinse well under cool running water, and pat dry with paper towels. Trim all fat and silverskin from the pork. Coat with the olive oil, and season with the pepper and chopped rosemary. Grill for a few minutes on each side. In a small bowl, combine the maple syrup and mustard. When the tenderloins are seared on all sides, brush them with the maple mustard mixture to coat. Loosely tent foil over the tenderloins and continue grilling until the internal temperature reaches 145°F. Allow to rest for 5 minutes before slicing.

To serve: Slice the pork and serve with the Caramelized Apples and Maple Mustard Sauce, garnished with rosemary sprigs.

Maple Mustard Sauce

This sauce can also be served with roasted chicken or turkey.

Yield: 2 cups

1 teaspoon olive oil
2 tablespoons minced shallots
1 tablespoon chopped fresh thyme
2 teaspoons freshly ground pepper
2 tablespoons white wine
1 cup double-strength chicken stock
2 tablespoons maple syrup
1 tablespoon Dijon mustard
2 tablespoons butter, softened

In a saucepan, heat the olive oil over medium-high heat, add the shallots, and sauté until golden. Add the thyme and pepper. Deglaze the pan with the white wine. Cook until the wine is reduced by half, and add the chicken stock. Reduce the heat to a simmer, and gently whisk in the maple syrup and mustard. Taste and adjust the seasonings. When ready to serve, whisk in the softened butter and serve with Grilled Pork Tenderloin with Caramelized Apples.

Apricot-Glazed Pork Tenderloin with Apricot Peach Chutney

This pork entrée is best at the height of summer when fresh apricots and peaches are available. For an unusual accompaniment, serve it with Almond Couscous Pilaf (see page 180). Give the couscous a flavorful boost by adding some of the extra juice drained from the chutney.

Yield: 6 servings

2 pork tenderloins, 12 ounces each, brined (see Basic Brine recipe, page 139)
¼ cup olive oil, divided
5 tablespoons apricot jam
2 tablespoons apple juice
6 sprigs fresh cilantro
Apricot Peach Chutney (recipe follows)

Preheat the oven to 400°F. Remove the tenderloins from the brine. Rinse well under cool running water, and pat dry with paper towels. Trim all fat and silverskin from the tenderloins. Coat with 2 tablespoons of the olive oil.

In a small saucepan over low heat, mix together the jam and apple juice. Heat until the jam is slightly thinned and brushable. In a large skillet over medium-high heat, heat the remaining 2 tablespoons of oil. When the oil is hot, sear the tenderloins, one at a time if there is not enough room in the skillet. Turn to sear them on all sides. Remove from the heat and place on a sheet pan.

Brush the tenderloins with the apricot glaze and bake until golden brown, 10 to 15 minutes. The internal temperature should be 145°F. Remove from the oven and allow to rest for 5 minutes before slicing. Serve garnished with fresh cilantro sprigs, passing the Apricot Peach Chutney separately.

Apricot Peach Chutney

You can serve this chutney warm or at room temperature. It is also a fine accompaniment for fish.

Yield: 2 cups

1 large peach, diced
2 fresh apricots, diced
⅓ cup diced red onion
1 tablespoon grated fresh ginger
¼ cup chopped fresh parsley
¼ cup chopped fresh cilantro
¼ cup rice wine vinegar
¼ cup brown sugar

In a large bowl, combine the peach, apricots, onion, ginger, parsley, and cilantro. Toss together to mix well.

In a small saucepan over medium-high heat, bring the vinegar to a boil, reduce the heat, add the brown sugar, and simmer until all the sugar has dissolved. Remove from the heat, and immediately pour the syrup over the fruit, onion, and herb mixture. Stir to combine, slightly cooking the fruit with the hot syrup. Serve with Apricot-Glazed Pork Tenderloin.

Almond-Crusted Pork Tenderloin with Lingonberry Ginger Relish

Most often associated with Scandinavia, lingonberries are also plentiful in Alaska's northern forests and tundra. Although we share nature's bounty with the local bear community, plenty remains for making sauce, chutney, and relishes.

Yield: 6 servings

3 eggs
2 tablespoons whole milk
2 cups fresh bread crumbs
6 tablespoons chopped dry-roasted almonds
1 tablespoon chopped fresh thyme
1 teaspoon freshly ground pepper
2 pork tenderloins, 12 ounces each, brined (see Basic Brine recipe, page 139)
2 tablespoons butter, melted
1 cup Lingonberry Ginger Relish (recipe follows)

Preheat the oven to 425°F. Crack the eggs into a large bowl. Whisk the milk into the eggs, and set aside. In a second bowl, combine the bread crumbs, almonds, thyme, and pepper, and set aside.

Remove the tenderloins from the brine. Rinse well under cool running water, and pat dry with paper towels. Trim all fat and silverskin from the tenderloins. Brush a sheet pan with the melted butter. Dip the tenderloins into the egg mixture, and then roll them in the bread crumb mixture, gently pushing the crust onto the tenderloin to coat. Set on the prepared sheet pan. Roast the tenderloins until they reach an internal temperature of 145°F and the crust has a nice golden color, 15 to 20 minutes. Allow them to rest for 5 minutes before slicing. Serve with Lingonberry Ginger Relish.

Lingonberry Ginger Relish

If lingonberries are not available, use fresh cranberries in this relish.

Yield: 2½ cups

2 cups fresh lingonberries, cleaned
2 cups sugar
½ cup cranberry juice
½ cup dried tart or sour cherries
⅓ cup rice wine vinegar
2 tablespoons crystallized ginger, minced
⅛ teaspoon ground ginger
⅛ teaspoon ground cinnamon
⅛ teaspoon cayenne
¼ cup apricot jam

In a large saucepan over medium-high heat, mix together the lingonberries, sugar, and juice. Bring to a rapid boil, reduce the heat, and simmer for 10 minutes. Add the cherries, vinegar, crystallized ginger, cinnamon, and cayenne. Continue simmering for 10 more minutes. Mix in the apricot jam. Remove from the heat and let cool to room temperature. Serve with Almond-Crusted Pork Tenderloin.

Salmon

Salmon has firm flesh and a delicate flavor, lending itself to many culinary applications. It can be smoked, poached, broiled, seared, baked, steamed, or grilled. Salmon can also be paired with a wide range of condiments, from the most simple, delicate butter sauces to more complex sauces and salsas. Unlike salmon most commonly consumed in the Lower 48 states, Alaska salmon is wild, not farm raised. The flavor of most farm-raised salmon tends to be more homogenous than the rich, sweet flavor of wild salmon. Even though wild salmon is more costly and harder to find, it is well worth the expense. Sockeye, king, chum, coho, and humpback are the five wild salmon species fished in our waters. At Camp Denali and North Face Lodge, we serve king salmon.

Barbecued Alaskan King Salmon

We barbecue our salmon as fillets with the skin on, so you will need a grill basket or fish rack. The skin helps retain juices, keeping the fish very moist. Fresh from the grill, salmon tastes great just as it is. We also like to dress it up a bit with the sauces that follow this basic recipe.

Yield: 6 servings

4 tablespoons butter
2 tablespoons margarine
2 pounds center-cut king salmon fillet, skin on, pin bones removed
2 teaspoons kosher salt
1 teaspoon garlic powder
1½ teaspoons freshly ground pepper
1 lemon, cut into 6 wedges
12 sprigs parsley

Light a grill. Fashion a tray out of a double thickness of aluminum foil, with ½-inch sides, large enough to fit your grill basket. Melt together the butter and margarine. Grease the bottom of the foil tray with some of the melted butter and margarine. Set the fish in the tray, skin side down. Brush some of the melted butter mixture over the fish, and season with the salt, garlic powder, and pepper. Using nonstick cooking spray, grease the grill basket very well.

Secure the fish, still in the foil tray, in the grill basket. Grill the fish, flesh side down, for about 10 minutes; the cooking time will depend on the thickness of the fillet. Flip the grill basket over, brush the fish with the melted butter mixture, cover the grill, and continue cooking. If your grill does not have a cover, loosely cover the grill basket with a sheet of aluminum foil. Grill skin side down for 3 to 5 minutes. Test the center of the fillet with the tip of a knife to ensure that it is cooked through. Carefully remove the fish from the grill basket and serve the fillet whole or portion it into the desired number of servings. Garnish with lemon wedges and parsley before serving.

Thai Black Bean Sauce for Salmon

This Thai-inspired sauce also works well as a vegetarian entrée when served with steamed basmati rice.

Yield: 4 cups

1 cup dried black beans
2 tablespoons olive oil
2 tablespoons dark sesame oil
1 tablespoon minced garlic
1 tablespoon grated fresh ginger
½ cup diced red bell pepper
½ cup diced green bell pepper
¼ cup rice wine vinegar
2 tablespoons honey
⅛ teaspoon cayenne
¾ cup pineapple juice
2 tablespoons cornstarch
2 tablespoons water
½ cup chopped fresh cilantro

Soak the beans overnight covered in cool water. The next day, rinse the beans well and drain. Transfer the beans to a large, heavy-bottomed stockpot, and cover again with cool water. Bring to a boil over medium-high heat. Reduce the heat and simmer until the beans are cooked tender, about 45 minutes. Strain and rinse the beans under cool running water.

In a large saucepan, heat together the olive and sesame oils over medium-high heat. Add the garlic and ginger, and sauté until aromatic. Add the red and green bell peppers, and sauté until tender. Deglaze the pan with the rice wine vinegar. Add the honey, cayenne, and pineapple juice. Simmer together to allow the flavors to combine. Add the cooked black beans.

In a small bowl, mix the cornstarch with the water, and slowly mix it into the black bean sauce. The addition of the cornstarch will make the sauce cloudy at first; simmer until the sauce is clear again and slightly thickened. Taste and adjust the seasonings. Just before serving, mix in the cilantro. Serve warm over grilled salmon.

Fresh Fruit Salsa for Salmon

The bold flavors of the mango and lime in this salsa pair wonderfully with the rich, smoky flavor of grilled salmon. You can use different fruit in this recipe to suit your taste, but always use the freshest and ripest fruit available. Make this salsa the day you plan to serve it.

Yield: 2 cups

1 mango, peeled and diced
2 kiwi fruit, peeled and diced
⅓ cup diced cantaloupe
4 large strawberries, hulled and diced
⅓ cup diced red onion
2 tablespoons fresh lime juice
2 teaspoons minced jalapeño chile
1 teaspoon kosher salt
½ cup chopped fresh cilantro

In a large bowl, mix all of the ingredients together. Cover and refrigerate for 2 to 4 hours. Allow the salsa to come to room temperature before serving. Mix it together again just before serving.

Ginger Plum Sauce for Salmon

This refreshing, simple sauce also works well with grilled lamb or veal.

Yield: 2 cups

6 plums, pits removed and diced
1 teaspoon grated fresh ginger
½ cup plum wine
2 tablespoons sugar
½ teaspoon kosher salt
¼ teaspoon red pepper flakes
½ cup chopped fresh mint
¼ cup chopped fresh cilantro
2 scallions, sliced on a slight diagonal

In a large bowl, mix together the plums and ginger. Set aside. In a small saucepan over medium-high heat, bring the wine to a boil and reduce by half. Add the sugar. Reduce the heat to low, and simmer until all of the sugar has melted. Remove from the heat and pour the syrup over the plums. Gently stir in the salt and red pepper flakes. Mix in the mint, cilantro, and scallions. Serve while still slightly warm.

Beef

Nothing says comfort food like steak and potatoes. At Camp Denali and North Face Lodge, we proudly serve Black Angus Certified Beef.

Pepper-Crusted Beef Tenderloin with Dijon Peppercorn Sauce

At our lodges we buy beef tenderloin whole, sear it, and then slice it for service. Because of the torpedo shape of the tenderloin, it naturally cooks unevenly. Having this range of doneness works great for us because the same tenderloin can accommodate those who prefer their meat well done and those who prefer it medium-rare. If you prefer an even doneness throughout, fold the tip end of the tenderloin under and tie it together with butcher's twine. If you are preparing this for only a few people, we suggest buying filets mignons, which are steaks cut from the tenderloin.

Yield: 8 servings

1 beef tenderloin, 4 pounds
2 tablespoons olive oil, divided
1 tablespoon coarsely cracked peppercorns
2 teaspoons kosher salt
2 tablespoons chopped fresh thyme
Dijon Peppercorn Sauce (recipe follows)

Preheat the oven to 400°F. Trim all fat from the tenderloin. Rub the tenderloin with 1 tablespoon of the olive oil. In a small bowl, combine the pepper, salt, and thyme. Rub the spice mixture into the tenderloin.

In a large skillet over medium-high heat, heat the remaining tablespoon of olive oil. When the oil is hot, sear the tenderloin on all sides, about 1 minute per side. Transfer the seared tenderloin to a sheet pan. Roast for 30 minutes. Check the internal temperature, and remove from the oven when the desired temperature is reached: 140°F for medium-rare, 155°F for medium, 165°F for well done. Allow the tenderloin to rest for 5 minutes before carving. Serve with Dijon Peppercorn Sauce.

Dijon Peppercorn Sauce

Mustard, sherry, and peppercorns are classic pairings for beef. This sauce is sure to impress, yet is very easy to make. It is best prepared right before serving.

Yield: 1 ½ cups, 8 servings

4 tablespoons butter, divided and softened
3 tablespoons chopped leeks
3 tablespoons dry sherry
1 tablespoon ground peppercorn mélange
1 tablespoon Dijon mustard
1 teaspoon beef au jus concentrate (if not available, use beef bouillon)
1 cup heavy cream

In a medium-size saucepan, melt 3 tablespoons of the butter over medium-high heat. Add the leeks and sauté until golden. Add the sherry and cook until reduced by half. Add the ground pepper, and reduce the heat to a simmer. Whisk in the mustard and au jus concentrate.

Slowly whisk in the heavy cream. Right before serving, swirl in the remaining 1 tablespoon of softened butter. Serve immediately over carved beef tenderloin.

Grilled Marinated Flank Steak

Flank steak comes from the rear section on the underside of the animal. It is a very lean, thin, and tasty cut of meat, usually weighing around 2 pounds. The marinade used for this grilled steak helps to form a tasty glaze on the beef. To match the bold flavors of the marinade, we serve flank steak with Roasted Garlic Smashed Potatoes accompanied by Seared Peppers and Onions with Molasses Balsamic Glaze (see pages 177 and 178).

Yield: 4 servings

1 flank steak, about 2 pounds
¼ cup orange juice concentrate
5 tablespoons soy sauce
¼ cup dark sesame oil
2 tablespoons crushed garlic
2 tablespoons grated fresh ginger

Trim all visible fat from the flank steak. In a small bowl, mix the remaining ingredients together. Pour into a glass or enamel casserole dish large enough to hold the flank steak. Set the flank steak in the marinade, cover, and refrigerate for 12 to 18 hours. Turn the steak once during the marinating time to ensure even flavoring.

Heat a grill. Remove the flank steak from the marinade. Grill, uncovered, until well browned on one side, 2 to 3 minutes. Turn over the steak and grill on the second side until well browned, 2 to 3 minutes. Remove the steak from the grill and let it rest for 5 minutes. Slice thinly on a slight diagonal against the grain.

Pan-Seared Filets Mignons with Merlot Sauce

Our Merlot Sauce has a deep, clear, ruby color that complements the dark brown exterior and tender pink interior of the filets. Serve this dish for an elegant holiday buffet. Simply sear a whole tenderloin, serving the sauce on the side.

Yield: 6 servings

6 filets mignons, 8 ounces each
2 teaspoons kosher salt
1 tablespoon chopped fresh rosemary
2 teaspoons freshly ground pepper
3 tablespoons olive oil
6 sprigs rosemary
Merlot Sauce (recipe follows)

Preheat the oven to 400°F. Trim all fat from the filets. Pat the filets dry with paper towels, and season with the salt, rosemary, and pepper.

In a large, heavy-bottomed skillet, heat the oil over medium-high heat. When it is hot, sear the filets on both sides, in batches if necessary, about 5 minutes per side. Transfer the seared filets to a sheet pan. Roast for 10 minutes. Check the internal temperature, and remove from the oven when the desired temperature is reached: 140°F for medium-rare, 155°F for medium, 165°F for well done.

Garnish with rosemary sprigs, and serve immediately with Merlot Sauce.

Merlot Sauce

This wine sauce can be made up to two days ahead of time. Reheat it before serving.

Yield: 2 cups

3 tablespoons water
¼ cup sugar
3 tablespoons red wine vinegar
3 tablespoons butter
1 cup minced shallots
2 cups merlot
2 cups demi-glace or rich veal stock
Salt and fresh ground pepper

In a small, heavy-bottomed saucepan, bring the water and sugar to a boil and cook, stirring, just until the sugar is dissolved. Once the sugar has dissolved, continue boiling without stirring until the mixture is a golden caramel. Remove the pan from the heat and carefully add the vinegar by pouring it down the side of the pan. The caramel will steam and harden. Return the pan to the heat and continue cooking, stirring to soften the caramel, for about 3 minutes. Remove from the heat and set aside.

In a second saucepan, melt the butter over medium-high heat. Add the shallots and sauté until golden. Stir in the merlot, bring to a boil, and reduce by half. Stir in the demi-glace or stock. Bring to a boil and cook until reduced to 2 cups, about 10 minutes. Remove from the heat and stir in the caramel. Pour the sauce through a sieve into a bowl. Season with salt and pepper. Serve with pan-seared filets, or refrigerate until needed.

Vegetarian Entrées

In many fine dining establishments, the vegetarian options on the menu seem to be a bit of an afterthought, usually consisting of nothing more than some combination of grains and greens. At Camp Denali and North Face Lodge, we celebrate vegetarian cuisine, offering an enlightened vegetarian option with each meal. The following are just a few of our favorite recipes. As we test out new menus, we are creating new vegetarian entrées all the time.

Corn, Cheese, and Chile Tamales

These tamales make a wonderful zesty meal when served with fresh fruit salsa and Coconut Rice (see page 176). Masa harina is a dough made from fire-dried corn kernels that have been cooked in limewater (water mixed with calcium oxide), and then ground into flour.

Yield: 18 tamales

1 (6-ounce) package dried corn husks
1 pound large poblano chiles
2 cups masa harina
6 tablespoons butter, softened
3 tablespoons sugar
2 teaspoons kosher salt
½ cup rich vegetable stock
5 cups frozen corn kernels, thawed and divided
3 cups grated sharp cheddar cheese, divided
1 teaspoon baking powder
1 teaspoon freshly ground pepper

Select the largest, sturdiest husks, and soak them in water, weighing them down with a plate to keep them covered. Set aside. Tear the remaining husks into ½-inch-wide strips to make 36 ties.

Using long tongs, char the chiles directly over a gas flame or in a broiler until blackened. Set in a medium bowl, cover tightly with plastic wrap, and let stand for 10 minutes. Peel, seed, and chop the chiles, and set aside.

Using a food processor, combine the masa harina, butter, sugar, and salt until the mixture forms a coarse meal. Add the vegetable stock and purée until smooth. Add 3 cups of the corn, 1 cup of the cheese, and the baking powder and pepper, pulsing the motor on and off until blended. Transfer to a large bowl, and stir in the remaining corn.

For each tamale, open 1 large softened husk. Place ⅓ cup of dough in the center of each husk. Make a depression in the dough and fill with 1 tablespoon of the chiles and 1 tablespoon of the remaining cheese. Using moistened fingertips, gently press the dough over the filling, shaping the dough into a log shape. Wrap the corn husk tightly around the filling, tying the ends tightly with the strips of husk. Repeat until all tamales are formed.

In a large pot with a steamer insert, place enough water to reach the bottom of the insert. Layer the tamales in the steamer insert. Bring the water to a boil over medium-high heat. Cover the pot and steam the tamales, adding more boiling water as needed, until they are firm, about 45 minutes. Serve the tamales warm in husks.

Goat Cheese Soufflé with Thyme

Soufflés are very easy to make and very impressive to serve. You can make this one even more special by serving individual portions prepared in 2-cup ramekins.

Yield: 4 servings

5 tablespoons butter, softened and divided
¼ cup grated Parmesan cheese
6 ounces goat cheese, crumbled
1 tablespoon chopped fresh thyme
½ cup all-purpose flour
1 cup whole milk
¼ cup dry white wine
1 tablespoon Dijon mustard
1 teaspoon kosher salt
1 teaspoon freshly ground pepper
4 egg yolks
10 egg whites
½ cup grated sharp cheddar

Preheat the oven to 375°F. Generously butter a 2-quart soufflé dish, using 1 tablespoon of the butter. Coat the inside of the dish with the Parmesan cheese and set aside.

In a medium saucepan, melt the remaining 4 tablespoons butter over low heat. Stir in the goat cheese, thyme, and flour and whisk until blended. Whisk in the milk, wine, and mustard. Continue cooking and whisking until the sauce is smooth and thick. Remove from the heat. Season with the salt and pepper. Stir in the egg yolks, scrape the soufflé mixture into a large bowl, cover with plastic wrap, and set aside. In a large stainless steel bowl, beat all 10 egg whites with a pinch of salt until soft peaks form. Fold the egg whites into the soufflé mixture. Using a large rubber spatula, gently scrape the soufflé mixture into the prepared dish. Sprinkle the cheddar cheese over the top. Bake in the center of the oven until nicely risen and golden brown, 25 to 30 minutes. Do not open the oven while baking, as this will cause the soufflé to fall. Remove from the oven and serve immediately.

Spring Vegetable Pot Pies

You can use different vegetables in these pies to suit the season and your personal taste.

Yield: 6 individual pot pies

Pot Pies
1 pound puff pastry, chilled
5 tablespoons butter, divided
6 baby red potatoes, diced
12 baby carrots, cut in half lengthwise
1 pound thin asparagus, cut into 1-inch lengths
12 cremini mushrooms, sliced
6 fresh shiitake mushrooms, sliced
2 teaspoons kosher salt
2 teaspoons freshly ground pepper
2 scallions, thinly sliced
6 large kale leaves, inner rib removed, chopped
1 cup frozen peas, slightly thawed
¼ cup chopped fresh chives
¼ cup chopped fresh parsley
1 tablespoon chopped fresh tarragon
1 tablespoon chopped fresh thyme
3 tablespoons all-purpose flour
3 cups rich vegetable stock, warmed
¾ cup heavy cream
1 tablespoon Dijon mustard

Egg Wash
1 egg yolk
1 tablespoon heavy cream

Preheat the oven to 400°F. Select 6 deep, ovenproof bowls or ramekins. Roll out the puff pastry to a thickness of ⅛ inch. Using one of the bowls or ramekins as a template, cut 6 rounds of pastry. Transfer the rounds to a sheet pan and refrigerate.

In a large, deep skillet, melt 2 tablespoons of the butter over medium-high heat. Add the potatoes and carrots and cook, stirring frequently, until soft, about 10 minutes. Add the asparagus and mushrooms and sauté until the asparagus is crisp and the mushrooms are tender. Season with salt and pepper. Add the scallions and kale, stirring to combine. Continue cooking until the kale is wilted. Stir in the peas, remove from the heat, and stir in the chives, parsley, tarragon, and thyme. Set aside.

In a medium saucepan, melt the remaining 3 tablespoons butter over medium-high heat. Add the flour and cook, whisking until blended. Slowly whisk in the warmed vegetable stock. Whisk in the heavy cream and mustard. Stir the sauce into the prepared vegetables, and allow to cool slightly.

To make the egg wash, in a small bowl whisk together the egg yolk with the cream.

Spoon the vegetable filling into the bowls. Brush the rim of each bowl with the egg wash. Carefully top each bowl with a puff pastry round, gently pressing it at the edges to seal. Brush the top of the pastry with the egg wash. Carefully set the bowls on a sheet pan lined with parchment paper and bake until the pot pies are puffed and golden, about 30 minutes. Remove from the oven and allow to cool for 2 minutes. Serve immediately.

Spicy Black Bean Cakes

The avocado and sour cream help cool the spiciness of these little cakes. Cooking the black beans in a rich vegetable broth infuses them with flavor.

Yield: 18 cakes, 6 servings

1 cup dried black beans
6 cups rich vegetable stock
6 scallions, thinly sliced
½ cup diced red bell pepper
½ cup chopped fresh cilantro
1 tablespoon minced garlic
1½ teaspoons minced jalapeño chile
1 tablespoon ground cumin
1 tablespoon kosher salt
2 eggs
¼ cup bread crumbs
1 cup yellow cornmeal
6 tablespoons olive oil
2 large avocados, peeled and pitted, each cut into 9 slices
6 tablespoons sour cream
18 sprigs cilantro

Soak the beans overnight covered in cool water. Rinse the beans well and drain. Transfer to a large, heavy-bottomed stockpot and add vegetable stock to cover. Bring to a boil over medium-high heat. Reduce the heat and simmer until the beans are cooked tender, about 45 minutes. Drain and rinse under cool running water.

Place the drained beans in a large bowl. Using a potato masher, mash the beans coarsely. Add the scallions, red bell pepper, cilantro, garlic, and jalapeño. Stir to combine well. Season with the cumin and salt, stirring to combine. Mix in the eggs, stirring to combine. Add the bread crumbs to form a dough. Place the cornmeal in a shallow bowl.

Scoop out 2 tablespoons of the bean mixture and drop it into the cornmeal, turning to coat. Shape into a cake and repeat with the remaining bean mixture, making a total of 18 cakes.

Preheat the oven to 250°F. In a large skillet, heat 3 tablespoons of the oil over medium-high heat. When the oil is very hot, start frying the bean cakes, working in batches. Fry for about 5 minutes per side. Drain the bean cakes on paper towels and transfer to a shallow baking dish. Keep them warm in the oven while frying the remaining cakes.

Serve the bean cakes warm on slices of avocado, topped with a dollop of sour cream. Garnish with cilantro sprigs.

Bulgur-and-Pine-Nut-Stuffed Tomatoes

Currants and lemon juice add a sweet tang to this dish, balancing well with the heartiness of the lentils, bulgur, and pine nuts.

Yield: 6 servings

Tomatoes
6 large tomatoes
2 teaspoons kosher salt, divided
2 tablespoons petite green lentils
1½ cups vegetable stock, divided
¼ cup olive oil
½ cup pine nuts
1 cup minced shallots
1 tablespoon minced garlic
½ cup bulgur
1 pound baby spinach
⅓ cup dried currants
1 teaspoon freshly ground pepper
½ cup grated Parmesan cheese
3 tablespoons chopped fresh parsley
2 tablespoons chopped fresh dill
2 tablespoons fresh lemon juice

Sauce
½ cup yogurt
½ cup sour cream
1 teaspoon grated lemon zest
2 teaspoons kosher salt
¼ teaspoon cayenne

Cut off and discard the top fourth of the tomatoes. Gently scoop out the insides, leaving the shell intact for the filling. Sprinkle the insides of the tomato shells with a total of 1 teaspoon of the salt, and drain upside down on a rack while preparing the filling.

In a small pot over medium-high heat, simmer the lentils with ½ cup of the vegetable stock until the lentils are tender, about 20 minutes. Drain and rinse well; set aside.

Preheat the oven to 350°F. In a medium saucepan with a lid, heat the oil over medium-high heat. Add the pine nuts and sauté until aromatic. Using a slotted spoon, transfer the nuts to a paper towel to drain. In the same saucepan, sauté the shallots and garlic, stirring occasionally, until soft. Add the bulgur and spinach, and sauté until the spinach has wilted. Add the remaining 1 cup vegetable stock and the currants. Add the cooked lentils and the pine nuts. Season with the remaining 1 teaspoon salt and the pepper. Remove from the heat, cover with the lid, and let stand until the bulgur is tender, about 30 minutes.

Stir the Parmesan cheese, parsley, dill, and lemon juice into the bulgur. Scoop into the prepared tomato shells. Set the tomatoes in a shallow casserole dish and bake until warmed through, 10 to 12 minutes.

To make the sauce: In a small bowl, mix together the yogurt, sour cream, lemon zest, salt, and cayenne. Transfer to a small serving bowl, and serve alongside the stuffed tomatoes.

Eggplant Napoleons

It is important to look for eggplant with a tight, dark skin that is free of blemishes. For this recipe, look for long, thin eggplant rather than the huge, pear-shaped variety.

Yield: 6 servings

½ cup olive oil
1 pound Japanese eggplant, cut crosswise into ⅓-inch slices
1¼ pounds zucchini, cut crosswise into ⅓-inch slices
4 large plum tomatoes, cut lengthwise into ⅓-inch slices
2 red onions, cut into ⅓-inch slices
1 pound red potatoes, cut into ⅓-inch slices
Kosher salt
Freshly ground pepper
1 cup ricotta cheese
1½ teaspoons fresh thyme
8 ounces mozzarella, cut into ¼-inch slices
6 sprigs rosemary

Preheat the oven to 450°F. Brush 2 sheet pans with some of the olive oil. Arrange as many of the vegetables as possible in a single layer in the pans. Brush the vegetables with some of the olive oil and season with salt and pepper. Roast the vegetables in the lower third of the oven until just tender and lightly browned, 10 to 15 minutes, rotating the pans halfway through. Transfer the roasted vegetables to a tray, arranging them by type in a single layer to cool. Roast the remaining vegetables in the same manner.

In a small bowl, stir together the ricotta and thyme. Season with salt and pepper.

Put 1 eggplant slice on a lightly oiled sheet pan. Spread 1 tablespoon of the ricotta mixture over the eggplant, top with 2 potato slices and then layer with 2 zucchini slices, 1 onion slice, 1 mozzarella slice, 2 tomato slices, 2 zucchini slices, and 1 additional onion slice. Spread a second tablespoon of the ricotta mixture over the last layer of onion, and top with 1 eggplant slice. Secure the tower with a bamboo skewer.

Repeat the process with the remaining vegetables, forming 5 more towers. Return to the oven for 5 minutes, until the vegetables are heated all the way through and the cheese has melted.

Trim the rosemary sprigs so that they are an inch taller than the Napoleons, and remove the bottom leaves from the sprigs, leaving about 1 inch of needles around the top. After removing the Napoleons from the oven, remove the bamboo skewers and replace them with the rosemary sprigs to serve.

Dolmades *(Stuffed Grape Leaves)*

You can find grape leaves sold in jars at most markets. A 16-ounce jar typically contains forty to sixty leaves. If you'll be serving these as a dinner entrée, count on four to six dolmades per person. They also make wonderful hors d'oeuvres. Dolmades can be prepared a few days in advance and served at room temperature.

Yield: 32 dolmades

½ cup olive oil
1 large yellow onion, diced
4 scallions, thinly sliced
1 tablespoon minced garlic
½ cup raw, long-grain rice
½ cup vegetable stock
¼ cup chopped fresh dill
¼ cup chopped fresh parsley
2 tablespoons fresh lemon juice
¼ cup pine nuts, toasted
1 teaspoon kosher salt
1 teaspoon freshly ground pepper
1 (16-ounce) jar grape leaves

In a large, heavy-bottomed skillet with a lid, heat the oil over medium-high heat. Add the onion and sauté until tender. Add the scallions and garlic, and sauté until aromatic. Add the rice, vegetable stock, dill, parsley, and lemon juice. Cover and simmer for 5 minutes. Remove from the heat (the rice will not be fully cooked), and stir in the pine nuts. Season with the salt and pepper. Allow to cool while preparing the grape leaves.

Remove the desired number of grape leaves from the jar. Rinse well, drain, and pat dry with paper towels. Using a sharp knife, cut the heavy stems from the leaves. Line a large sauté pan with a few grape leaves and set aside.

To roll the dolmades, set a grape leaf on a work surface, rough side up, with the stem end nearest you. Set a well-rounded teaspoon of the rice mixture near the stem end. Using both hands, fold the leaf over the rice mixture, fold both ends in, and continue rolling tightly toward the tip of the leaf. Set in the prepared pan and repeat with the remaining leaves and rice mixture, nesting the dolmades tightly in the pan. When the pan is full, add enough water to cover the dolmades, bring to a boil over medium-high heat, reduce the heat, cover the pan, and cook at a bare simmer for ½ hour. Check to make sure the rice is tender. Serve warm or at room temperature.

Side Dishes

These wonderful accompaniments are in no way less important than the featured entrée in creating a truly great meal. Whatever you choose to serve with a featured entrée should bring balance to the plate, enhancing the flavor, texture, and presentation of the whole meal.

White Beans with Tomatoes and Garlic

These beans are fully flavored and very savory. They pair wonderfully with lamb and chicken but are just as satisfying on their own. If you find yourself with any left over, they make a great base for a hearty, healthy bean soup.

Yield: 4 cups

1½ cups dry white beans
5 cups rich chicken stock
2 tablespoons olive oil
⅓ cup diced red onion
1 tablespoon minced garlic
1 pound diced ripe Roma tomatoes
2 teaspoons kosher salt
1 teaspoon freshly ground pepper
¼ cup chopped fresh parsley
2 tablespoons grated lemon zest

Soak the beans overnight covered in cool water. Rinse well and drain. Transfer the beans to a large, heavy-bottomed stockpot, and add the chicken stock. Bring to a boil over medium-high heat. Reduce the heat and simmer until the beans are cooked tender, about 45 minutes. Drain the beans and rinse them under cool running water. Set aside.

In a large, 2-inch-deep sauté pan, heat the olive oil over medium-high heat. Add the onion and garlic, and sauté until golden. Add the tomatoes, stirring to incorporate. Sauté for 1 minute to release some of the juice. Reduce the heat and stir in the white beans. Season with the salt and pepper. Simmer together for 10 minutes. Stir in the parsley and lemon zest, and remove from the heat. Taste and adjust the seasonings before serving.

Asparagus with Brown Butter

Browning the butter adds a rich, nutty flavor to the asparagus. Look for asparagus that is thin and firm.

Yield: 6 servings

1½ pounds asparagus
1 tablespoon table salt
4 tablespoons butter
2 teaspoons grated lemon zest
1 teaspoon kosher salt
1 teaspoon freshly cracked pepper

Fill a large stockpot with water, add the table salt, and bring to a boil over high heat. Snap the tough ends off the asparagus. Fill a large bowl with ice and water, and set aside. Plunge the asparagus into the salted boiling water. Cook until just tender and the color is bright green. Immediately drain the asparagus into a colander, and then plunge it into the ice water to cool. In a skillet large enough to hold the asparagus, melt the butter over medium-high heat. Keep it over the heat until the butter starts to brown. Watch this carefully, as it can burn very fast. When the butter is nicely browned, add the lemon zest and then the asparagus, gently shaking the pan to coat the asparagus in brown butter. Season with the kosher salt and pepper.
Serve warm or at room temperature.

Wild Rice Cakes

We serve these with pork tenderloin, but the nutty, slightly smoky flavor of the rice can be served alongside any type of game bird. Wild rice takes much longer to cook than other types of rice. For this recipe you can make the rice a day ahead of time, store it in the refrigerator, and bring it to room temperature before forming and frying the cakes.

Yield: 8 servings (16 cakes)

3 cups rich vegetable stock
1½ cups uncooked wild rice
2 tablespoons minced garlic
¼ cup chopped fresh chives
½ cup dry white bread crumbs
2 eggs, beaten
1 cup vegetable oil

In a medium saucepan with a lid, bring the vegetable stock to a boil over high heat. Add the wild rice, cover, and reduce the heat to a bare simmer. Cook, covered, for 1 hour. Uncover and test the rice for doneness. Add some water and continue cooking if needed. Set the rice aside to cool.

In a medium-size bowl, mix together the garlic, chives, and bread crumbs. Add the rice, and mix well. Add the eggs, a little at a time, until the mixture starts to hold together. In a large skillet over high heat, heat ½ cup of the oil until almost smoking. Carefully drop small scoops, about 2 tablespoons per scoop, of rice mixture into the hot oil. Do not crowd the pan. Fry for 1 minute, then gently turn over the cakes and fry for 1 minute more. Using a slotted spoon, remove the cakes from the oil, drain on paper towels, and repeat with the remaining rice mixture, adding oil as needed to maintain oil level in pan. Serve warm.

Grilled Radicchio

When slightly grilled, radicchio picks up a smoky flavor and a subtle sweetness. Although we recommend grilling it directly on a charcoal, wood, or gas grill, a grill pan works well in a pinch.

Yield: 8 servings

4 medium heads radicchio
¼ cup olive oil
1 tablespoon kosher salt
1 tablespoon freshly ground pepper
2 tablespoons honey

Heat a grill. Cut each radicchio head into quarters. Wash well, keeping the quarters intact. Drizzle the oil over the radicchio, turning to coat. Sprinkle the salt and pepper over the radicchio. Grill, cut side down, for 2 minutes, until slightly marked by the grill. Turn carefully and grill the other cut side. Drizzle the honey over the grilled side of the radicchio. Continue grilling until slightly tender. Carefully remove the radicchio from the grill, keeping the quarters intact. Serve warm or at room temperature.

Lemon Parsley Orzo Pasta

Orzo is a very small, grain-shaped pasta, often confused with rice because of its similar shape and size.

This is a very versatile side dish. The simple, clean, fresh flavors make it easy to pair with chicken, fish, meat, or vegetarian entrées.

Yield: 6 servings

1 pound orzo pasta
⅓ cup extra-virgin olive oil
¼ cup minced garlic
¼ cup grated lemon zest
2 teaspoons kosher salt
2 teaspoons red pepper flakes
1 cup chopped fresh parsley
8-ounce chunk Parmesan cheese

Bring a large pot of lightly salted water to a boil over medium-high heat. When it reaches a rapid boil, add the pasta. Cook until al dente, testing often. Drain the pasta in a tight mesh strainer. Rinse with cold water to stop the cooking.

While the pasta is cooking, heat the oil in a medium-size sauté pan over medium-high heat. Add the garlic and sauté until golden. Reduce the heat to low and add the lemon zest, salt, and red pepper flakes. Toss in the cooked pasta, stirring to combine. Add the parsley. Slice the cheese, using a vegetable peeler. Serve the pasta warm or at room temperature, garnished with thick slices of Parmesan cheese.

Baby Bok Choy with Soy Ginger Sauce

Bok choy is a loose-leafed green Chinese cabbage with white ribs. It grows in a bulb form, and is almost entirely white at the base and very leafy green at the top. Baby bok choy is harvested when the cabbage is very young. It is delicate and tender with a very sweet, watery taste.

Yield: 6 servings

6 heads baby bok choy
2 tablespoons olive oil, divided
2 teaspoons kosher salt
2 teaspoons freshly ground pepper
Soy Ginger Sauce (recipe follows)

Preheat the oven to 425°F. Slice the bok choy in half lengthwise. Wash well, keeping the halves intact. Oil a sheet pan or shallow casserole dish with 1 tablespoon of the olive oil. Set the bok choy, cut side down, in the pan or dish. Drizzle the remaining 1 tablespoon oil over the bok choy. Season with the salt and pepper. Bake for 7 to 10 minutes. The leaves should be slightly wilted and the base of the bok choy should be tender to the touch. Using a pastry brush, coat the bok choy with warm Soy Ginger Sauce. Serve immediately.

Soy Ginger Sauce

This versatile sauce is a fine accompaniment to a variety of vegetables or to rice.

Yield: ½ cup

1 teaspoon dark sesame oil
1 teaspoon olive oil
1 teaspoon minced garlic
1 teaspoon grated ginger
2 tablespoons soy sauce
2 tablespoons water
½ teaspoon rice wine vinegar
1 teaspoon honey
2 tablespoons thinly sliced scallions
1 teaspoon sherry
1 teaspoon cornstarch

In a small saucepan, heat the sesame and olive oils over medium-high heat. Add the garlic and ginger and sauté until very aromatic. Add the soy sauce, water, vinegar, and honey. Bring to a boil, then reduce the heat. Add the scallions. In a small cup, combine the sherry and cornstarch. Whisk into the sauce. Simmer for a few minutes, until the sauce thickens slightly and clears. Use immediately.

Potato Slims

Because they are baked rather than fried, these potatoes are a healthier alternative to the classic steak fries.

Yield: 6 servings

2 large Idaho (russet) potatoes, unpeeled
5 tablespoons butter
¼ teaspoon Tabasco sauce
2 cups saltine cracker crumbs
2 teaspoons garlic salt

Preheat the oven to 375°F. Slice each potato into 12 long wedges. Rinse well under cool running water, and allow to air-dry on a clean dish towel. In a small saucepan, melt the butter over medium-high heat. Add the Tabasco sauce, and remove from the heat. In a medium bowl, mix together the cracker crumbs and garlic salt.

Dip the potatoes into the seasoned butter, and then into the seasoned cracker crumbs, coating the potatoes well. Set the potatoes, skin side down, on a sheet pan. Bake for 1 hour, then check for doneness. The coating should be crisp and golden brown. When you slice into the center of a wedge, the inside should be soft and cooked through. Serve immediately.

Coconut Rice

This is a very aromatic, tasty rice dish. Cooking the rice in stock intensifies its flavor.

Yield: 6 servings

1 tablespoon olive oil
1 tablespoon butter
2 cups basmati rice
2 cups coconut milk
2 cups chicken stock
1 teaspoon ground ginger
2 kefir lime leaves (optional)
½ teaspoon red pepper flakes
½ cup unsweetened shredded coconut, toasted

In a medium-size saucepan with a lid, heat together the olive oil and butter over medium-high heat. Add the rice and sauté for 3 minutes. Add the coconut milk, and stir to combine. Add the chicken stock, ginger, lime leaves, if using, and red pepper flakes; stir to combine. Bring to a boil, then reduce heat to low. Cover and simmer for 20 minutes. Test to make sure the rice is tender. Remove the lime leaves, and stir in the toasted coconut.

Seared Peppers and Onions with Molasses Balsamic Glaze

Serving these with our Grilled Marinated Flank Steak (see page 153) complements their bold, savory flavor.

Yield: 4 servings

½ large red onion
1 red bell pepper, seeded
1 yellow bell pepper, seeded
1 green bell pepper, seeded
1 tablespoon olive oil
2 tablespoons molasses
1 tablespoon balsamic vinegar
2 teaspoons kosher salt
2 teaspoons coarsely ground pepper
2 teaspoons chopped fresh thyme

Slice the onion in half, then into 6 long wedges. Slice each red and green bell pepper into 8 long wedges. In a large, 2-inch-deep skillet, heat the olive oil over medium-high heat. Add the onion and sauté for 1 minute. Add the bell pepper wedges and sauté for 1 minute more. Add the molasses and balsamic vinegar, stirring to coat. When the peppers are tender, remove the pan from the heat. Season with salt, pepper, and thyme, and serve warm.

Roasted Garlic Smashed Potatoes

We refer to these as smashed potatoes because they are just coarsely mashed with the back of a spoon. Roasting the garlic gives it rich flavor and makes it easier to digest. Roasted garlic is a great food to have on hand. You can keep it refrigerated for up to two weeks.

Yield: 6 servings

Roasted Garlic
1 large head garlic
1 teaspoon olive oil
1 teaspoon kosher salt

Potatoes
4 tablespoons butter
¼ cup heavy cream
14 small red potatoes, washed
1 tablespoon salt
1 tablespoon freshly ground pepper

To make the roasted garlic: Preheat the oven to 350°F. Cut the tapered end off the head of garlic, very near the top, exposing the cloves. Drizzle the oil onto the cut end of the garlic, allowing it to seep in. Sprinkle the salt on top of the oil. Wrap the garlic tightly in foil and roast it for about 45 minutes. Test it by squeezing gently on the foil; the garlic should be very tender. Remove from the oven, and allow to cool before unwrapping the foil.

To prepare the potatoes: In a small pan, over low heat, melt together the butter and cream; keep warm.

Set the potatoes in a large pot, and add water to cover. Bring to a boil over medium-high heat. Boil the potatoes until tender, about 20 minutes. Insert a fork into the center of a potato to check doneness; the potato should easily fall off the fork. Quickly drain the potatoes and return them to the same pot. Add the warmed butter and cream. Smash the potatoes into the butter and cream with the back of a spoon. Unwrap the garlic and squeeze the roasted cloves out of their skins into the smashed potatoes. The roasted garlic should be fork tender. Continue mashing and smashing with the spoon. The potatoes should be slightly mashed, with larger chunks of potatoes and skin still visible. Season with salt and pepper.

Sautéed Zucchini and Summer Squash with Oven-Dried Tomatoes

Oven-drying the tomatoes intensifies their flavor.

Yield: 6 servings

Tomatoes
3 Roma tomatoes, quartered
1 tablespoon olive oil
1 teaspoon dried oregano
1 teaspoon dried basil
2 teaspoons kosher salt
1 teaspoon freshly ground pepper

Zucchini and Summer Squash
1 tablespoon olive oil
1 teaspoon minced garlic
2 zucchini, sliced 1-inch thick on the diagonal
2 summer squash, sliced 1-inch thick on the diagonal
1 teaspoon kosher salt
1 teaspoon freshly ground pepper
3 tablespoons chiffonade (thin strips) of fresh basil

To dry the tomatoes: Preheat the oven to 350°F. In a medium bowl, gently toss together the tomatoes and olive oil. Season with the oregano, basil, salt, and pepper. Spread the tomatoes out in a single layer, skin side down, on a sheet pan lined with parchment paper. Bake for 30 to 45 minutes. The tomatoes will have reduced dramatically in size and will be slightly dry to the touch.

To sauté the zucchini and summer squash: In a large sauté pan, heat the oil over medium-high heat. Add the garlic and sauté until golden. Add the zucchini and summer squash, and season with salt and pepper. Sauté until tender and lightly browned. Remove from the heat. Toss in the oven-dried tomatoes, and serve garnished with the basil chiffonade.

Almond Couscous Pilaf

Couscous, sometimes mistaken for a grain, is in fact tiny balls of dough made from a paste of ground grains and water. This North African staple has found its way into mainstream cuisine. The turmeric in this dish colors the couscous a bold yellow.

Yield: 6 cups

2 tablespoons olive oil
¼ cup minced shallots
1 tablespoon minced garlic
2 cups uncooked couscous
2 cups rich vegetable stock
½ teaspoon ground turmeric
2 teaspoons kosher salt
1 cup toasted almonds, chopped
3 Roma tomatoes, diced
1 cucumber, peeled, seeded, and diced
½ cup chopped fresh cilantro
1 tablespoon fresh lemon juice
1 teaspoon honey
¼ cup pineapple juice

In a large saucepan with a lid, heat the oil over medium-high heat. Add the shallots and garlic. Sauté until golden, and then add the couscous. Stir to coat the couscous with oil. Add the vegetable stock, turmeric, and salt. Bring to a boil, remove from the heat, cover, and let stand until the couscous is tender, about 10 minutes.

Using a large fork, gently toss the almonds, tomatoes, cucumber, and cilantro with the couscous. In a small bowl, whisk the lemon juice, honey, and pineapple juice together. Using the fork, gently toss the juice mixture into the couscous pilaf, a little at a time, until the pilaf is moist. Taste and adjust the seasonings.

The Grand Finale

Our bakers start from scratch using the best-quality chocolate couveratures, organic flour, grains, nuts, and the ripest, freshest fruit to create these contemporary classics.

Rustic Nectarine-and-Plum Galette

Cream cheese in the tart dough gives it a very delicate crumb and at the same time makes it a bit easier to work with than an all-butter tart dough.

Yield: One 10-inch galette, 10 servings

Tart Shell
½ cup sugar
5 tablespoons butter, softened
½ teaspoon vanilla extract
2 tablespoons (1 ounce) cream cheese
1 egg
2 cups all-purpose flour
¼ teaspoon salt

Filling
5 plums, halved and pitted, each half cut into 6 slices
5 nectarines, halved and pitted, each half cut into 6 slices
½ teaspoon ground ginger
6 tablespoons sugar, divided
1 tablespoon all-purpose flour
2 tablespoons butter, melted
1 egg, whisked to blend
¼ cup apricot preserves

To make the tart shell: Using an electric mixer fitted with the paddle attachment, mix together the sugar, butter, vanilla, and cream cheese until light and fluffy. Slowly incorporate the egg. With the mixer on low speed, quickly add the flour and salt. Mix just until a dough forms. Gather the dough into a ball and gently press it into a disk. Wrap in plastic wrap and freeze for 1 hour.

To make the filling: Preheat the oven to 400°F. In a large bowl, toss together the plums, nectarines, ginger, and 4 tablespoons of the sugar.

To assemble and bake the tart: Remove the dough from the freezer. Roll it out on a lightly floured surface into a 14-inch round. Transfer to a sheet pan lined with parchment paper. Mix 1 tablespoon of the remaining sugar with the flour and sprinkle it over the dough, leaving a 2-inch border at the edge. Leaving the 2-inch border plain, arrange the nectarines and plums in alternating concentric circles, working from the outside toward the center. Drizzle the melted butter over the fruit. Fold the dough border in toward the center of the tart. Brush the exterior of the border with the whisked egg, and sprinkle the border with the remaining 1 tablespoon sugar. Bake until the fruit is tender and the crust is a golden brown, about 45 minutes. In a small saucepan over low heat, melt the apricot preserves until thin, and brush over the top of the tart. Allow the tart to cool on the sheet pan for 1 hour. Run a long, thin knife under the tart to loosen it. Carefully transfer it to a serving platter, or cut it into the desired portions and serve from the pan.

Chocolate Roulade

This lighter-than-air, melt-in-your-mouth chocolate dessert with subtle orange overtones will delight anyone who has a passion for chocolate.

Yield: 12 servings

Cake
6 ounces high-quality bittersweet chocolate
3 tablespoons water
6 large eggs, separated
⅔ cup superfine sugar, divided
¼ teaspoon salt
1 tablespoon unsweetened cocoa powder (preferably Dutch process)

Filling
1 cup heavy cream
2 tablespoons powdered sugar
1 tablespoon Grand Marnier
1 teaspoon grated orange zest
2 tablespoons unsweetened cocoa powder

To make the cake: Preheat the oven to 350°F. Oil a 15-by-10-by-1-inch shallow jelly roll pan. Line the bottom of the pan lengthwise with a large piece of waxed or parchment paper, letting the paper hang slightly over the ends. Coarsely chop the chocolate.

In a heavy-bottomed sauté pan, melt the chocolate and water together over low heat, stirring continuously until smooth. Remove from the heat and cool. Using an electric mixer, beat the egg yolks with ⅓ cup of the sugar until light and pale. The egg yolks should leave a ribbon trail when the beater is raised. Fold in the melted chocolate until blended.

Using a very clean bowl and clean beaters, beat the egg whites with the remaining $\frac{1}{3}$ cup sugar and the salt until they hold stiff peaks. Fold $\frac{1}{3}$ of the stiff egg whites into the chocolate mixture to lighten it. Gently fold in the remaining egg whites, mixing gently until thoroughly combined. Spread the batter evenly in the prepared pan. Bake in the center of the oven until puffed up and dry to the touch, 15 to 18 minutes.

Transfer the pan to a cooling rack, and cover the top of the cake with layers of slightly dampened paper towels. Let stand for 5 minutes, then remove the towels. Run a thin blade between the cake and the sides of the pan. Sift 1 tablespoon of cocoa powder over the top of the cake, then overlap 2 sheets of waxed paper lengthwise over the cake. Flip over the cake, remove the pan, and gently peel off the layer of waxed paper covering the base of the cake.

To make the filling and fill the cake: Using an electric mixer, beat together the cream, powdered sugar, and Grand Marnier until the mixture just holds stiff peaks. Fold in the orange zest. Gently spread the filling evenly over the cake. Set a platter long enough to hold the roulade right next to the long side of the cake. Using waxed paper as an aid, gently roll up the cake lengthwise. Carefully transfer the roulade, seam side down, to the platter. Dust the top generously with 2 tablespoons of cocoa. Serve or refrigerate.

Classic New York–Style Cheesecake

A great cheesecake should be rich and creamy, with a smooth, light texture. Many people tend to overcook cheesecake, which gives it an unpleasant granular texture. Do not worry if the cheesecake still looks slightly loose when removed from the oven. It will set up as it cools. We allow at least eight hours between baking and serving our cheesecakes.

Yield: 12 servings (one 9-inch cheesecake)

Crust
9 tablespoons butter, softened, divided
⅔ cup chopped pecans
1½ cups gingersnap crumbs
1½ cups graham cracker crumbs

Filling
3 pounds cream cheese
2 cups sugar
1 tablespoon vanilla extract
2 eggs
2 egg yolks
2½ tablespoons cake flour
½ cup sour cream

To make the crust: Generously butter the sides of a 9-inch springform pan, using 1 tablespoon of the butter. Lightly butter the bottom of the pan and line it with parchment paper. Sprinkle the pecans onto the sides of the pan, turning the pan to coat the sides evenly. Using a food processor, combine the gingersnap and graham cracker crumbs with the remaining 8 tablespoons butter, pulsing the machine on and off until the crumbs hold their shape when squeezed together. Using the base of a glass, press the crumb mixture into the bottom of the pan, coating it evenly.

To make the filling: Preheat the oven to 300°F. Using an electric mixer fitted with the paddle attachment, combine the cream cheese and sugar. Beat together until light, fluffy, and lump free, stopping to scrape down the bowl and beater twice while mixing. Slowly incorporate the vanilla, eggs, and yolks. Mix together well on low speed. Slowly mix in the cake flour. Using a spatula, fold in the sour cream. Pour into the prepared pan. Set the pan on a sheet pan lined with parchment paper.

Bake in the center of the oven about 1 hour and 15 minutes, until the top is puffed up and slightly golden in color. Turn off the oven and allow the cheesecake to continue baking in the oven for 20 minutes as it cools. Remove the cheesecake from the oven. Leave it in the pan and let it cool to room temperature. Refrigerate. Allow the cheesecake to set up for 8 hours before serving.

Variations on Classic New York–Style Cheesecake

Options for flavoring and topping cheesecake are limitless. Here are a few of our favorites.

Chocolate Espresso Cheesecake

Use 3 cups Oreo cookie crumbs for the bottom crust, omitting the gingersnap and graham cracker crumbs. In a double boiler, melt 5 ounces semisweet chocolate with 3 tablespoons butter and 3 tablespoons strong espresso. Make the cheesecake filling as directed in the main recipe. After folding in the sour cream, fold in the chocolate mixture.

Pumpkin Cheesecake

Use 3 cups gingersnap cookie crumbs for the bottom crust, omitting the graham crackers. Make the cheesecake filling as directed in the main recipe. After folding in the sour cream, fold in 1 can (16 ounces) pumpkin purée and 1 teaspoon mixed ground spices (ginger, cloves, allspice, nutmeg, and cinnamon).

Cardamom Chocolate Almond Cheesecake

Coat the sides of the pan with finely chopped almonds instead of pecans. Use 3 cups cardamom cookie crumbs for the bottom crust, omitting the gingersnap and graham cracker crumbs. In a double boiler, melt 5 ounces dark semisweet chocolate with 3 tablespoons butter and 2 teaspoons almond extract. In a small bowl, mix together 1 teaspoon ground cinnamon, ½ teaspoon ground cardamom, and ¼ teaspoon ground ginger.

Make the cheesecake filling as directed in the main recipe. After folding in the sour cream, fold in the chocolate mixture and the spice mixture.

Fruit-Topped Cheesecake

Make and bake a cheesecake, following the main recipe. In a medium saucepan over medium-high heat, combine ¼ cup sugar with 1 tablespoon arrowroot and 2½ cups fresh or frozen fruit, thawed. If using previously frozen fruit, add only ¼ cup of the juice. Add 1 teaspoon fresh lemon juice. Simmer until the sauce is clear and slightly thickened. Remove from the heat; and spread while warm on the cooled cheesecake.

Citrus Cheesecake

Mix together 2 tablespoons grated lemon zest, 2 tablespoons grated lime zest, and 2 tablespoons sugar. Use this mixture in place of the chopped nuts to line the sides of the pan. Use 3 cups lemon- or lime-flavored cookie crumbs for the bottom crust, omitting the gingersnaps and graham cracker crumbs. Substitute 1 tablespoon Key lime juice for the vanilla extract.

Strawberry-Rhubarb Crisp

Rhubarb is one of the only perennial food plants hardy enough to survive winters in our outside garden. This crisp is best served warm, complemented by a small scoop of hand-cranked vanilla ice cream.

Yield: 6 servings

Topping
1 cup brown sugar
¾ cup all-purpose flour
¾ cup rolled oats
2 teaspoons ground cinnamon
1 teaspoon ground nutmeg
1 teaspoon ground ginger
1 teaspoon grated orange zest
¼ pound (1 stick) butter, cubed
1 teaspoon vanilla extract

Filling
1½ cups white sugar
2 cups fresh strawberries, hulled and quartered
3 tablespoons cornstarch
1 teaspoon butter
4 cups chopped fresh rhubarb

Preheat the oven to 400°F. Lightly grease a 9-inch round baking pan, 2 inches deep.

To make the topping: Using a food processor, combine the brown sugar, flour, oats, cinnamon, nutmeg, ginger, and orange zest, pulsing the machine on and off. Add the butter and vanilla and continue to pulse until the mixture resembles a lumpy streusel topping. Set aside.

To make the filling: In a large bowl, mix together the sugar, strawberries, and cornstarch, tossing to coat the berries. Melt the butter in a large saucepan over medium-high heat. Add the rhubarb and sauté until slightly tender. Remove from the heat and add the warm rhubarb to the strawberry mixture.

Pour the fruit into the prepared pan. Sprinkle the topping over the fruit. Set the pan in a larger pan to catch any juices that overflow while baking. Bake until the topping is golden brown and the fruit juices are bubbling, 30 to 50 minutes. If the topping is getting too browned before the fruit is cooked, loosely tent it with foil and continue baking. Allow the crisp to cool for 30 minutes before serving.

Chocolate Mousse

By definition, all mousses are composed of eggs and egg whites, as well as cream, sugar, flavorings, and chocolate or fruit. The eggs for mousse are not cooked all the way through, so we use eggs that have been separated and pasteurized before packaging. These are hard to find for home use, however. For home preparation, we recommend using organic, naturally nested, free-range eggs.

Yield: 8 cups

6 eggs, separated
1 cup sugar
2½ cups heavy cream
¼ cup unsweetened cocoa powder
¾ cup warm water
¼ cup dark rum
8 ounces semisweet chocolate, melted
¼ cup light corn syrup

Fill the bottom of a double boiler with warm water. Bring to a simmer over medium-high heat. Whisk the egg whites and sugar together in the top of the double boiler set over the simmering water. Whisking continuously, bring the meringue mixture to 140°F. Remove from the heat, transfer to the bowl of an electric mixer fitted with the whisk attachment, and whip at high speed until completely cooled. Set the meringue aside.

Whip the heavy cream to stiff peaks and refrigerate until ready to use.

Mix the cocoa powder into the warm water, add the rum, and then mix in the melted chocolate. Keep warm until ready to use.

In a clean bowl use an electric mixer fitted with the clean whisk attachment, whisk the egg yolks to break them up. In a small pan over medium-high heat, bring the corn syrup to a boil. With the mixer running, gradually add the hot corn syrup to the egg yolks. Whip until the mixture is thick and fluffy. Fold the warm chocolate mixture into the egg yolks. Fold this mixture into the reserved whipped cream, and gradually add this mixture to the reserved meringue. Cover and store in the refrigerator for 30 minutes before serving.

Lemon Torte

Lemon desserts are especially refreshing. At the height of summer, garnish this torte with fresh, sweet berries.

Yield: One 9-inch torte, 10 servings

Crust
1 cup all-purpose flour
⅓ cup powdered sugar
¼ pound (1 stick) butter, cubed and chilled

Filling
⅔ cup fresh lemon juice
½ cup white sugar
5 eggs
4 tablespoons butter, cubed
½ teaspoon vanilla extract

Topping
⅔ cup cake flour
4 tablespoons butter, cubed and chilled
⅓ cup white sugar
½ teaspoon baking powder
⅓ cup sliced almonds

Preheat the oven to 350°F. Lightly grease a 9-inch springform pan.

To make the crust: Using an electric mixer fitted with the paddle attachment, mix the flour and powdered sugar together. Cut in the butter until the mixture is crumbly. Press into the bottom of the prepared pan. Bake for 15 minutes, until the crust is light golden. Set aside to cool.

To make the filling: Reduce the oven temperature to 340°F. In a heavy-bottomed saucepan over medium-high heat, bring the lemon juice and sugar to a simmer, dissolving the sugar. In a large bowl, lightly whisk the eggs. Gradually add the lemon syrup to the eggs, whisking constantly to combine. When all the syrup has been added, return the mixture to the saucepan, reduce the heat, and continue to cook, stirring constantly, until very thick. Remove from the heat and mix in the butter and vanilla. Set aside to cool slightly.

To make the topping: Using an electric mixer fitted with the paddle attachment, mix together the cake flour, butter, sugar, baking powder, and almonds. Combine until the mixture resembles a crumbly streusel topping.

To assemble and bake the torte: Gently spread the lemon filling over the baked crust. Sprinkle the topping over the filling, and return the pan to the oven. Bake for an additional 30 minutes, until the topping is golden brown and the filling is set. Let cool in the pan for 30 minutes. Run a thin blade between the edge of the torte and the side of the pan before releasing the spring. Serve at room temperature or slightly chilled.

Decadent Carrot Cake

The following recipe is a simple base for a great, classic carrot cake. If you enjoy fruit (such as bananas, pineapple, or apples) or nuts (such as pecans, macadamia nuts, or walnuts) in your carrot cake, fold them into the batter when you add the carrots. We serve this cake with Bittersweet Fudge Sauce, which complements the ginger and cinnamon.

Yield: One 10-inch cake, 10 servings

Cake
4 eggs
¾ cup vegetable oil
2 teaspoons vanilla extract
2 cups white sugar
½ teaspoon salt
3 cups whole wheat pastry flour
1½ tablespoons ground cinnamon
1 tablespoon ground ginger
1½ teaspoons baking soda
¼ teaspoon baking powder
1 pound carrots, peeled and shredded

Frosting
1¼ cups (10 ounces) cream cheese
4 ounces white chocolate, melted
1 teaspoon vanilla extract
6 tablespoons butter, softened
2 tablespoons grated orange zest
1½ cups powdered sugar
2 cups hazelnuts, toasted and chopped
2 cups shredded sweetened coconut, toasted
Bittersweet Fudge Sauce (recipe follows)

To make the cake: Preheat the oven to 375°F. Lightly grease a 10-inch round cake pan. Using an electric mixer fitted with the whisk attachment, whip the eggs until light and frothy. Slowly incorporate the oil and vanilla, and then slowly add the sugar and salt. In a separate bowl, mix together the flour, cinnamon, ginger, baking soda, and baking powder. Add the flour mixture to the egg mixture. Fold in the carrots. Pour the batter into the prepared pan. Bake the cake in the center of the oven for 45 minutes, or until it springs back when pressed lightly in the center. Let rest in the pan for 10 minutes, then run a thin blade around the sides of the cake, invert it onto a cooling rack, and remove the pan. Allow to cool completely before frosting.

To make the frosting: Using an electric mixer fitted with the paddle attachment, beat the cream cheese on low speed until smooth. Gradually add the white chocolate, beating on low speed until smooth. Add the vanilla, butter, and orange zest, beating on low speed until smooth. Gradually add the powdered sugar, beating on low speed until smooth.

To frost the cake: Set the cake on a secure base, like the bottom of a springform pan or a cardboard cake round. Using an offset icing spatula, spread frosting over the sides and top of the cake. Keeping the cake on the base of a springform pan or a plate, hold the cake up with one hand, and with your other hand gently press the nuts and coconut into the frosting around the side wall of the cake. Refrigerate for 30 minutes before serving. Serve with Bittersweet Fudge Sauce.

Bittersweet Fudge Sauce

This is simply the best chocolate sauce ever. It complements the spices in the carrot cake, is wonderful when served over vanilla ice cream, and adds just the right touch of decadence to the Pumpkin Torte. Refrigerate extra sauce in a covered container for up to one month.

Yield: 1½ cups

6 ounces bittersweet chocolate
¼ cup unsweetened cocoa powder (preferably Dutch process)
1 cup water
⅔ cup sugar
2 tablespoons corn syrup
1 teaspoon vanilla extract

Break the chocolate into small pieces, place in a large bowl, and set aside. Place the cocoa powder in a second large bowl. In a saucepan over medium-high heat, bring the water, sugar, and corn syrup to a boil. Remove from the heat and stir in the vanilla. Slowly whisk enough of the syrup into the cocoa powder to form a thick paste. Whisk in the remaining syrup. Return the entire mixture to the saucepan. Bring the mixture to a boil, whisking constantly. Remove from the heat and pour over the chocolate. Allow the mixture to stand for 3 minutes to melt the chocolate. Whisk the mixture until smooth. When cool, store in an airtight container.

Pumpkin Torte

We are flooded with recipe requests whenever we serve this dessert. You will be impressed at how easy it is to prepare this wonderful torte.

Yield: One 10-inch torte, 12 servings

Cake Base
1¾ cups packaged yellow cake mix
5 tablespoons plus 1 teaspoon butter, melted
1 egg

Filling
3 cups pumpkin purée
⅓ cup light brown sugar
1 teaspoon ground cinnamon
1 teaspoon ground ginger
½ teaspoon ground nutmeg
¼ teaspoon ground cloves
2 eggs
⅔ cup heavy cream

Topping
1 cup packaged yellow cake mix
3 tablespoons butter, softened
1 teaspoon ground cinnamon

Bittersweet Fudge Sauce (optional)

Preheat the oven to 350°F. Grease a 10-inch springform pan well.

To make the cake base: Using an electric mixer fitted with the paddle attachment, mix together the cake mix, butter, and egg. Combine well. Press into the bottom of the pan, using lightly floured fingertips to spread the mixture evenly.

To make the filling: In a large bowl, mix together the pumpkin purée, brown sugar, cinnamon, ginger, nutmeg, cloves, eggs, and cream. Mix until smooth. Pour the pumpkin mixture over the cake layer.

To make the topping: Using an electric mixer fitted with the paddle attachment, mix together the second cake mix, butter, and cinnamon until the mixture resembles a lumpy streusel topping. Sprinkle over the pumpkin layer.

Bake for 45 minutes, until the topping is a golden brown and a toothpick inserted in the center of the cake comes out clean. Let cool in the pan for 20 minutes. Run a thin blade around the edge of the torte to loosen it before releasing the spring. Continue to cool completely before serving. Serve with Bittersweet Fudge Sauce (page 196), if desired.

Flourless Chocolate Cake

Chocolate lovers delight at this intensely rich and decadent dessert. This is a very simple dessert to make, but once out of the oven lack of flour makes it extremely fragile. It must be cut when chilled and is best served at room temperature.

Yield: One 9-inch cake, 12 servings

2 teaspoons butter, melted
1 tablespoon unsweetened cocoa powder
6 ounces semisweet chocolate
7 ounces unsweetened chocolate
10 tablespoons water
1 cup plus 2 tablespoons white sugar, divided
½ pound (2 sticks) butter, cubed
6 eggs
2 tablespoons powdered sugar
1 pint fresh raspberries
2 cups sweetened whipped cream

Preheat the oven to 325°F. Brush the inside of a 9-inch springform pan with the melted butter. Dust the buttered pan with the cocoa powder. Set aside.

Coarsely chop the semisweet chocolate and unsweetened chocolate into small pieces. In a medium-size saucepan over high heat, bring the water and ¾ cup sugar to a rapid boil, and remove from the heat. Stir in the chocolate until melted. Stir in the butter until melted and completely incorporated. Set aside at room temperature.

Using an electric mixer fitted with the whisk attachment, whip the eggs with the remaining ¼ cup plus 2 tablespoons sugar at high speed until light and fluffy. Very gently fold the chocolate mixture into the egg mixture until completely incorporated.

Pour the batter into the prepared pan. Bake in the center of the oven for 25 minutes. The top should feel firm to the touch, not tacky. Remove from the oven, and allow the cake to cool to room temperature in the pan on a cooling rack. Then refrigerate the cake, still in the pan, for 2 hours before unmolding. Run a thin blade around the edge of the cake before releasing the spring. Sprinkle the powdered sugar over the cake, and serve with fresh raspberries and whipped cream.

All-American Shortcakes

The blueberries, red strawberries, and white whipped cream all topped with a star-shaped shortcake make this a great dessert to serve on the Fourth of July.

Yield: 8 servings

Shortcakes
2 cups all-purpose flour
1 tablespoon baking powder
¼ teaspoon salt
5 tablespoons sugar, divided
¼ pound (1 stick) butter, cubed and chilled
1 egg, lightly beaten
½ cup half-and-half
1 tablespoon butter, melted
1 tablespoon grated lemon zest

Topping
2 cups strawberries, hulled and sliced
2 cups blueberries, stemmed
2 cups blackberries
5 tablespoons sugar
2 tablespoons crème de cassis (black currant liqueur)
2 cups sweetened whipped cream

To make the shortcakes: Preheat the oven to 425°F. Using a food processor, pulse together the flour, baking powder, salt, and 3 tablespoons of the sugar. Scatter the cubed butter over this mixture, tossing to coat it with the flour. Cut the butter into the flour mixture using quick, 1-second pulses, until the flour mixture is pale yellow and resembles cornmeal. Turn the mixture out into a medium-size bowl. Mix the egg and half-and-half together, and pour into the bowl with the flour mixture.

Using a stiff rubber spatula, stir together the mixture just until a dough starts to form. Turn the dough out onto a lightly floured surface. Using a floured rolling pin, gently roll the dough out to about ½-inch thick. Dip a 2-inch round biscuit cutter and a similar-size star cookie cutter into a small amount of flour, and cut 8 cakes of each shape.

Line a sheet pan with parchment paper. Transfer the shortcakes to the pan, spacing them 1 inch apart. If they stick to the work surface, slide an offset spatula under them to loosen. Brush the tops of the stars with melted butter, and sprinkle with lemon zest and the remaining 2 tablespoons sugar. Bake until golden brown, 12 to 14 minutes. Cool in the pan on a cooling rack until ready to serve.

To make the topping: In a large bowl, mix together the strawberries, blueberries, blackberries, sugar, and crème de cassis. Let the mixture stand for at least 30 minutes to allow the fruit to release some juice, stirring occasionally. To serve, place the round cakes on individual plates, top with a portion of the berries and syrup and a dollop of whipped cream, and stand the star in the whipped cream.

CAMP DENALI
Classics

With each season that passes at Camp Denali and North Face Lodge, our recipe cache continues to grow. Our menus have changed over time to include available new foods, as well as new culinary trends. Some recipes, however, have remained tried and true through the years. This chapter is dedicated to some of those timeless classics.

Potato-Crusted Sausage Quiche

The potato crust helps make this a hearty and nutritious breakfast entrée. For a vegetarian version, substitute 1 cup lightly sautéed vegetables for the sausage.

Yield: 8 servings

Potato Crust
1 pound russet potatoes
1 egg
3 tablespoons all-purpose flour
½ teaspoon salt
¼ cup minced yellow onion
2 tablespoons butter, melted and divided

Filling
8 ounces bulk pork sausage
2 eggs
¼ teaspoon freshly ground pepper
1 cup evaporated milk
1 tablespoon all-purpose flour
1 clove garlic, minced
1½ cups grated cheddar cheese
1 tablespoon chopped fresh parsley

To make the potato crust: Preheat the oven to 350°F. Without peeling the potatoes, grate them into a bowl of cold water. Swirl to release some of the starch. Pour the grated potatoes into a strainer, rinse well, and drain. Wring out any excess moisture with a clean towel, and transfer the potatoes to a clean bowl. Mix in the egg, flour, salt and onion. Generously butter a 9-inch pie pan, using 1 tablespoon of the melted butter. Press the potato mixture into the pie pan, building up a rim on the sides, to form a crust. Bake for 15 minutes. Remove from the oven, brush the inside of the crust with the remaining melted butter, return to the oven, and continue baking for an additional 10 minutes.

While the crust is baking, prepare the filling: In a heavy-bottomed skillet over medium-high heat, sauté the sausage until browned. Remove from the heat and drain off the fat. In a medium-size bowl, whisk together the eggs, pepper, milk, flour, and garlic.

Spread the browned sausage on the bottom of the baked crust, sprinkle the grated cheddar cheese on top, pour the egg mixture over the cheese, and top with the chopped parsley. Return to the oven and bake for 30 to 40 minutes, until the center is set and the top is golden brown. Let cool and set for 10 minutes before cutting.

Hot Artichoke Dip

This dip also makes a terrific sandwich spread.

Yield: 3 ½ cups, 8 to 10 servings

1 cup grated Parmesan cheese
½ cup mayonnaise
½ teaspoon dried dill weed
1 clove garlic, minced
1 (14-ounce) jar marinated artichoke hearts, drained
1 cup (8 ounces) cream cheese, softened

Preheat the oven to 400°F. Using a standard blender, on medium speed, blend together the Parmesan cheese, mayonnaise, dill, garlic, and artichoke hearts. Scrape down the sides of the blender and blend again. Once the mixture is thoroughly combined, blend in the cream cheese, just to incorporate. Spread the mixture in a shallow-sided ovenproof dish, and set the dish in a larger pan to catch any drips. Bake until the top is golden and bubbly, about 15 minutes. Serve immediately with your favorite crackers.

Anadama Bread

This hearty bread claims New England heritage. The wife of a Yankee fisherman served him only cornmeal mush with molasses. Weary of this fare, he mixed it with flour and yeast, baked it as a bread, and exclaimed, "Anna, damn her!"

Yield: 2 loaves

½ cup cornmeal
½ cup cold water
1¼ cups boiling water
¼ cup vegetable oil
2 tablespoons honey
½ cup molasses
2 teaspoons salt
½ cup wheat germ
1 cup golden raisins
¼ cup powdered milk
1½ tablespoons active dry yeast
¼ cup warm water
3 to 4 cups all-purpose flour

In a large, heavy-bottomed saucepan, stir together the cornmeal and cold water. Continuing to stir, add the boiling water. Cook over medium-high heat, stirring constantly, until the mixture thickens. Remove from the heat, stir in the vegetable oil, honey, molasses, salt, wheat germ, raisins, and powdered milk, and mix until well combined.

In the bowl of an electric mixer fitted with the dough hook, dissolve the yeast in the warm water, allowing it to become frothy. With the mixer on low speed, gradually add the cornmeal mixture. Continue mixing, adding flour as needed, until a soft, smooth, elastic dough has formed. Turn out into an oiled bowl, turning the dough to coat it with oil. Cover and let rise in a warm place until almost doubled in volume.

Gently punch down the dough and turn it out onto a lightly floured work surface. Divide the dough in half and shape into 2 loaves. Place in greased loaf pans, cover, and let rise in a warm place until almost doubled in volume.

Preheat the oven to 350°F. Bake the loaves for 40 to 45 minutes. Remove from the oven and allow the bread to rest in the pans for 5 minutes, then remove from the pans to cool. Allow the bread to cool for at least 20 minutes before slicing.

Vegetarian Lasagna

For the best flavor, we recommend making the sauce a day ahead.

Yield: 12 servings

Sauce
1 tablespoon olive oil
1 yellow onion, minced
2 cloves garlic, minced
1 green bell pepper, minced
¼ cup chopped celery leaves
½ cup chopped fresh parsley
2 cups prepared tomato sauce
2 large tomatoes, diced
1 (6-ounce) can tomato paste
2 teaspoons dried oregano
2 teaspoons dried basil
1 bay leaf
½ teaspoon freshly ground pepper
2 teaspoons salt
⅛ teaspoon cayenne
1 teaspoon Worcestershire sauce

Lasagna
1 (8-ounce) package lasagna noodles
2 cups ricotta cheese
1 pound spinach, cooked and well drained
2 cups sliced fresh mushrooms
1½ cups sliced zucchini
8 ounces Monterey Jack cheese, grated
8 ounces mozzarella cheese, grated
1 large carrot, peeled and grated
½ cup sliced black olives
1 cup grated Parmesan cheese

To make the sauce: In a large saucepan, heat the oil over medium-high heat. Add the onion, garlic, and bell pepper. Sauté until aromatic. Stir in the celery leaves and parsley. Sauté until aromatic. Reduce the heat and stir in the tomato sauce, diced tomatoes, tomato paste, oregano, basil, bay leaf, pepper, salt, cayenne, and Worcestershire sauce. Simmer until very thick, up to 4 hours. Taste and adjust the seasonings. Cool and refrigerate until ready to use. Remove the bay leaf before using.

To assemble and bake the lasagna: Preheat the oven to 350°F. Lightly grease a deep-sided 9-by-13-inch baking dish, or extend the sides of a shallower pan with a double thickness of greased aluminum foil.

Spoon ⅓ of the sauce in the bottom of the dish, and top with a layer of uncooked lasagna noodles. Spread the ricotta cheese evenly over the noodles, and top with the spinach, mushrooms, and zucchini. Spoon ⅓ of the sauce over the top, and layer with the remaining noodles. Cover the noodles with the grated Monterey Jack and mozzarella cheeses. Top with the carrots and olives. Spoon the remaining sauce on top. Cover loosely with greased aluminum foil. Bake for 45 minutes, remove the foil, and continue to bake for an additional 30 minutes. Remove from the oven and top with the Parmesan cheese. Bake for 15 more minutes, until the cheese is golden brown and the sauce is bubbly. Remove the pan from the oven, and allow the lasagna to set for at least 15 minutes before cutting.

Chicken Phyllo Roll

When working with phyllo, it is best to keep it loosely covered with a few damp paper towels to keep it from drying out.

Yield: 6 servings

¼ cup vegetable oil
1 yellow onion, minced
2 cups sliced fresh mushrooms
1 pound spinach, cooked and well drained
2 cloves garlic, minced
4 ounces Gouda cheese, cubed
6 ounces sharp cheddar cheese, cubed
1 pound boneless, skinless chicken breast, cooked and diced
1 (10-ounce) can cream of mushroom soup
2 eggs, lightly beaten
1 (16-ounce) package phyllo, thawed
⅜ pound (1½ sticks) butter, melted
1 egg, lightly beaten

Preheat the oven to 350°F. In a heavy-bottomed skillet over medium-high heat, heat the oil. Add the onion and sauté. Add the mushrooms and sauté until tender. In a large bowl, mix together the spinach, garlic, Gouda, cheddar, chicken, mushroom soup, and eggs. Mix in the sautéed mushrooms and onions.

Lay a clean dish towel on a flat surface. Start stacking the phyllo, brushing each sheet with butter, until the stack is 10 layers deep. Spread half of the filling across the short width of the dough, about 5 inches from one end and 2 inches from each side edge. Fold the edges of the phyllo over the filling. Carefully roll the phyllo up over the filling, using the towel for support. Transfer to a sheet pan lined with parchment paper. Repeat the process with the remaining phyllo and filling. Brush the tops of the rolls with the beaten egg. Bake for 40 minutes, until the phyllo is crispy and golden brown. Let the phyllo rolls set for 10 minutes before slicing.

Sour Cream Halibut

This is a great recipe for any delicate white fish. It keeps the flesh of the fish extremely moist while infusing it with a rich, creamy flavor.

Yield: 6 servings

2 pounds halibut fillet
5 tablespoons butter
2 tablespoons fresh lemon juice
2 teaspoons lemon pepper
2 cups sour cream
½ cup mayonnaise
½ cup yogurt
1 cup finely ground cracker crumbs
2 teaspoons paprika
1 lemon, cut into 6 wedges

Preheat the oven to 375°F. Cut the halibut fillet into serving-size pieces. In the bottom of a 9-by-13-inch baking dish, melt the butter. Stir in the lemon juice. Arrange the fish in the baking dish and sprinkle with the lemon pepper.

In a small bowl, mix together the sour cream, mayonnaise, and yogurt, and spoon onto the fish. Bake for 20 minutes, remove from the oven, and top with the cracker crumbs. Sprinkle with the paprika. Bake for an additional 15 minutes, until the crumbs are a golden brown and the fish is firm and flakes easily. Serve garnished with lemon wedges, spooning extra sauce from the baking dish over the fish.

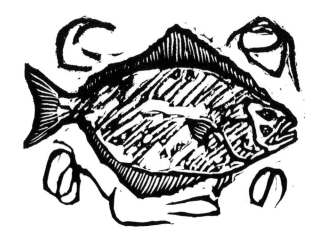

Navajo Tacos

An all-time staff favorite, this zesty chili is served up with all the usual taco accompaniments on a pillow of deep-fried dough.

Yield: 8 servings

Tacos
1½ pounds ground beef
1 tablespoon olive oil
1 yellow onion, diced
1 clove garlic, minced
1 green bell pepper, diced
1 (28-ounce) can diced tomatoes in juice
1 bay leaf
2 tablespoons chili powder
1½ teaspoons salt
⅛ teaspoon cayenne
¼ teaspoon paprika
1 tablespoon ground cumin
1 (15-ounce) can kidney beans, rinsed well and drained
Fried Dough Rounds (recipe follows)

Suggested Accompaniments
Chopped fresh cilantro
Shredded lettuce
Diced tomatoes
Chopped red onion
Grated cheddar cheese
Sour cream
Chopped scallions
Sliced black olives
Sliced avocado
Salsa

In a large, heavy-bottomed skillet, brown the ground beef in the olive oil, add the onion and garlic, and sauté until aromatic. Add the bell pepper, and sauté until tender. Stir in the tomatoes and their juice, bay leaf, chili powder, salt, cayenne, paprika, and cumin. Reduce the heat, cover, and simmer for 2 hours, adding water as needed to retain the consistency of a thick soup. Prepare the Fried Dough Rounds while the chili simmers.

Add the beans, and simmer for 15 additional minutes. Remove and discard the bay leaf. Place the Fried Dough Rounds on plates and top each with a hearty scoop of chili. Have the accompaniments available for each person to use to taste.

Fried Dough Rounds for Navajo Tacos

These fried breads also make an excellent dessert when tossed in cinnamon sugar right after frying.

Yield: 10 to 12 rounds

2 cups warm water
½ cup sugar
1 tablespoon active dry yeast
6½ to 7½ cups all-purpose flour, divided
⅓ cup powdered milk
¼ pound (1 stick) butter, softened
2 eggs
1 teaspoon salt
8 cups vegetable shortening for frying

In the bowl of an electric mixer, combine the warm water, sugar, and yeast. Let stand for a few minutes until the yeast is frothy. Fit the mixer with the dough hook. With the mixer on low speed, add 3½ cups of the flour and the powdered milk, and mix until a smooth consistency is reached. Add the butter, eggs, and salt, and mix until smooth. Gradually add the remaining flour as needed, mixing until a soft, smooth, elastic dough has formed. Turn out into an oiled bowl, turning the dough to coat it with oil. Cover and let rise in a warm place until almost doubled in volume.

Gently punch down the dough and turn it out onto a lightly floured work surface. Divide the dough in half, roll out each half to a ¼-inch thickness, cover, and let the dough relax for 10 minutes.

Preheat the oven to 250°F. In a deep, heavy-bottomed skillet or saucepan, heat the shortening until very hot, registering 360°F on a deep-fat thermometer. Cut the dough into 4-inch rounds, using a 4-inch bowl, lid, or biscuit cutter. Working in batches, carefully drop the dough rounds into the hot shortening, frying them on each side until puffed and golden brown. Drain on paper towels to absorb excess oil. Keep warm in the oven while frying the remaining dough.

Russian Cream

This light and tasty dessert is delicious topped with fresh berries.

Yield: 6 servings

½ cup sugar
2 teaspoons unflavored gelatin
½ cup water
1 cup heavy cream
1½ cups sour cream
1 teaspoon vanilla extract

   In a small saucepan, mix the sugar with the gelatin, and stir in the water. Bring to a boil over medium-high heat, stirring constantly. Remove from the heat and stir in the cream. Cover and refrigerate until thickened. Using an electric mixer fitted with the whisk attachment, whip together the sour cream and vanilla. Whip in the gelatin/cream mixture. Refrigerate until set. Spoon into serving dishes and keep chilled until ready to serve.

Muldrow Mud Cake

Originally known as "Mud Cake," this rich, moist chocolate dessert gradually assumed the namesake of the longest glacier on the north side of the Alaska range. It begins on Mount McKinley and its terminal moraine is a fascinating hiking destination for the more strenuous adventurers among our guests.

Yield: 12 servings

Cake
1 tablespoon unsweetened cocoa powder
1½ cups strong coffee or espresso
¼ cup coffee-flavored liqueur
5 ounces unsweetened baking chocolate
½ pound (2 sticks) butter, cubed
2 cups sugar
2 cups cake flour
1 teaspoon baking soda
¼ teaspoon salt
2 eggs
1 teaspoon vanilla extract

Chocolate-Espresso Glaze
4 ounces (¾ cup) semisweet chocolate chips
1 tablespoon butter
2 tablespoons strong coffee or espresso

To make the cake: Preheat the oven to 275°F. Generously grease a bundt cake pan. Dust the pan with the cocoa powder and set aside.

In a small saucepan over medium heat, combine the coffee or espresso and liqueur. Bring to a boil, reduce the heat, and stir in the chocolate and butter. Keep stirring until the chocolate is melted and the mixture is smooth. Add the sugar, stirring until dissolved. Remove from the heat and cool to lukewarm.

In a clean bowl, sift together the cake flour, baking soda, and salt. In a separate bowl, whisk together the eggs and vanilla. Gradually add the chocolate mixture to the flour, alternating with the eggs to avoid any lumps. Mix until the consistency is even and smooth. Pour the batter into the prepared pan, tapping it gently to remove any air bubbles.

Bake in the center of the oven for 90 minutes, until the cake pulls away slightly from the sides of the pan and the center springs back when touched. If you are using a very deep pan, insert a toothpick into the center of the cake. It should come out clean if the cake is done. Let the cake cool in the pan for 5 minutes to set, then invert the pan onto a cooling rack, tapping it gently if needed to loosen the cake. Remove the pan and allow the cake to cool slightly while preparing the glaze.

To make the glaze: In the top of a double boiler over medium-high heat, melt together all of the ingredients for the glaze, whisking to ensure a smooth consistency. When the desired consistency is reached, pour the glaze over the cake. Allow the cake and glaze to cool slightly before serving.

Homemade Hand-Cranked Ice Cream

If you have ever cranked your own ice cream, you know what a fun group activity it is. Hand cranking also produces the creamiest ice cream. It is a camp tradition, and it's only fair that the crankers get the first taste. The following recipe is for a 4-quart hand-crank freezer. For smaller home freezers, just cut the recipe to suit.

Yield: 2½ quarts, 12 servings

4 cups whole milk
1½ cups sugar
¼ teaspoon salt
3 eggs
4 cups heavy cream
1 tablespoon vanilla extract

Scald the milk in a heavy-bottomed stockpot over low heat, taking care not to let it boil. Remove from the heat and stir in the sugar and salt until all of the grains have dissolved. In a large bowl, whisk the eggs until frothy. Slowly whisk in half of the scalded milk mixture. Return the mixture to the stockpot and simmer over low heat, whisking constantly, until the mixture thickens. Remove from the heat and stir in the cream and vanilla. Pour the mixture into a 4-quart ice cream container. Cool to lukewarm. Churn in an ice cream freezer according to the freezer instructions.

INDEX

INDEX